COACH ANTONY BIRKS

SMALL TALK - Enlightening Interruptions

The importance of Small Talk in our business and private lives

Copyright © 2019 by Coach Antony Birks

All rights reserved. No part of this publication may be reproduced, stored or transmitted in any form or by any means, electronic, mechanical, photocopying, recording, scanning, or otherwise without written permission from the publisher. It is illegal to copy this book, post it to a website, or distribute it by any other means without permission.

Coach Antony Birks asserts the moral right to be identified as the author of this work.

Coach Antony Birks has no responsibility for the persistence or accuracy of URLs for external or third-party Internet Websites referred to in this publication and does not guarantee that any content on such Websites is, or will remain, accurate or appropriate.

Designations used by companies to distinguish their products are often claimed as trademarks. All brand names and product names used in this book and on its cover are trade names, service marks, trademarks and registered trademarks of their respective owners. The publishers and the book are not associated with any product or vendor mentioned in this book. None of the companies referenced within the book have endorsed the book.

For "fair use" as brief quotations embodied in articles and reviews, without the prior written permission of the copyright holder.

Your support of the authors' rights is appreciated.

The author of this book does not dispense medical advice or prescribe the use of any technique or method as a form of treatment for physical or medical problems without the advice of a physician, either directly or indirectly.

The intent of the author is to merely offer information of a general nature to help the reader in his or her quest for emotional wellbeing.

In the event the reader uses any of the information in this book, which is your constitutional right, the author can assume no responsibility for your actions.

First edition

ISBN: 9781097920655

Cover art by Cover Photo: Kuttelvaserova Stuchelova 332156234

This book was professionally typeset on Reedsy.
Find out more at reedsy.com

DEDICATION

Anne S, Marie-Laure F, Arthur W, Ute K, Albina I, Karlheinz B,
Christine Z, Sebastien R, Roland R, Judith R, Katharina F, Odile G,
Witali L, Thomas B, Angelika B, Jean-Paul G, Jean-Marie G,
Katharina H, Gennadij S, Virginie P, Ortwin F, Robert H,
Bastian W, Michael F, Jeannette K, Veronique G, Landry C,
Lionel G, Denis G, Elodie R, Christophe A, Francoise A,
Louis-Marie d-C,
Richard V, Fabrice T, Jean-Luc H, Nans L, Katharina W,
Veronique M, Philipp F, Petra G. and Naima e-K.

Contents

Acknowledgement	ii
NOTE FROM THE AUTHOR	v
INTRODUCTION	1
WHAT THE HELL IS SMALL TALK, ANYWAY?	9
WHY THEN, IS SMALL TALK SO HARD BUT IMPORTANT?	15
BUILDING TRUST & SHARING PERSONAL INFORMATION	33
DRESS CODE, EYE CONTACT & THE POWER OF TOUCH	39
NAME CALLING, THE SMILE & AN OPEN HAND	45
THE GOOD, THE BAD & THE UGLY TOPICS	51
CULTURAL AWARENESS, AGE & GENDER BIAS	67
TYING UP LOOSE ENDS	79
REFERENCES	94
About the Author	103
Also by Coach Antony Birks	106

Acknowledgement

I acknowledge and share the complexity of small talk - regardless of whatever level or acceptance we find ourselves in – together with its uses and methodologies.

This can be challenging – however, without undertaking this act of small talk, our lives cannot be truly whole and complete – so ultimately, we can move on and set ourselves free.

<u>I would first like to acknowledge **Andrea** for her patience, caring and love.</u>

The following people also contributed to the finished product found in this book:

      Stephi H.
      Pham
    Margit C. & Dieter C.
     Ben B. & Miles B.
      Linda A. [RIP]
     Annalena M. [RIP]

I would also like to acknowledge my friends and foes – past and present – who I willingly and whole-heartedly dedicate this book
... and forgive them ... through the process of writing this book.

SMALL TALK
(Enlightening Interruptions)
a
discussion
by
Coach Antony Birks

(2019)

The importance of
SMALL TALK
in our business and private lives

A Conversation

Coach Antony Birks

NOTE FROM THE AUTHOR

There have been many excellent books written about the topic of small talk … and to be honest, most are pretty good. Although, this particular book on small talk should perhaps be read firstly, as a conversation about the subject as a whole, why English is the language of small talk and after that, hopefully, a practical and useful guide.

It is not a definitive piece of writing … despite this, and as with most relationships, we are all on a continuous learning curve; and precisely because of this … we grow as people, a society or a civilisation; which hopefully makes us … stronger, better and in some ways … "more"!

Whatever your opinion might be about this subject, my wish at the start is that you read the following pages with an open and yet curious mind. I have striven to keep this book short and concise – mainly because an ever-increasing trend is for shorter books, owing perhaps to our fast-paced world, together with our frustratingly hectic lifestyles – described and spoken about in detail in my second book: Reaching Holistic Change.

This book also strives to be, for the most part, light-hearted in nature (as to be expected do most of my other books). I also understand that you, my dear reader, certainly have enough on your plate, so - if you are reading this in your spare time - I want you to enjoy and relish the process of reading these pages - the way you would enjoy an ice-cream on a hot summer's day.

First and foremost, there is a caring, respect and empathy for the reader; and because of this, there is something that makes this book different and perhaps unique – both in conception and certainly during the actual writing process.

We know instinctively that we cannot please everyone all of the time, because, as human beings, we are all uniquely different – and this is something to be celebrated. On many occasions, I feel the necessity to remind, even the mature students, of this understanding. Rather than being fearful of our uniqueness; we should instead, be rejoicing it; maybe even courageously sharing our uniqueness with others – perhaps via small talk?

This book is certainly not going to make you become the best small-talker unless firstly, you want this transformation to happen, and secondly that you practise and incorporate the ideas into your daily life.

I should also point out at the start that I come to this topic from a viewpoint that when I am not teaching my students Business English, I am coaching a diverse section of the population. Some might feel a little threatened because I am apparently criticising the way you are - by offering my opinions and observations about the subject matter – but this is not my intent. This book is merely the conglomeration of the retold stories and experiences gained during the last fifty-odd years of my life, through my teaching, coaching and just living in our modern, complicated and fast moving world.

I do talk a lot about respect, being curious, empathic and even being an ambassador (when travelling to other places, cultures and meeting people we do not know). What other people choose to do, is just that … their business. As explained more fully in my previous books, we can only do our best, at any stage of our lives; and, as life is ongoing in nature, we hopefully learn and then incorporate these experiences into our next (ad)ventures.

This, moreover, is not a guarantee that sincerely using the techniques in this book will always work – as mentioned previously, you are perhaps not that important, in the eyes of other people – no matter how close you think you are.

The people you meet regularly or encounter daily, be it a colleague, boss, family member, or friend, all have their own problems, concerns and lives to lead. Nevertheless, most feel they would rather be somewhere else – working for a different company; having a more understanding partner; living in a warmer climate; or having more money than they do today.

In my experience, we must first accept the tenet that change is normal; it is not only normal but just a significant part of life and that basically we are just … where we are. Now, if that last statement is factually correct and you can accept it, then it is our "reason for being" or *raison d'etre* for us to make the most of it – regardless if it now suddenly appears or feels not to be going the way we had first planned or intended.

Life is brimming full of the ups and downs, together with the difficulties of just existing in the modern world. Being resilient and remaining positive in those "down moments" and continuing, is undoubtedly the key or solution to living a healthy, happy life. Small talk is the enlightening interruptions of everyday life and I want you to enjoy these little pleasures.

My own personal experience has shown that we always have the choice to think another thought when doing something, and it is our interpretation or perception of what we think and believe, which is most significant. This is similar to an on/off switch – positive or negative – because, we as humans, can only think one thought at any one time.

It is NOT the responsibility of any other – be that partner, spouse, boss, client or colleague – to make us happy, regardless of the relationship we have with that person. Yet the social interaction between everyone we encounter, can/could/might potentially be something incredibly special and long-lasting. As mentioned later, we just have to give it a chance; expect the best and look forward to something new.

I have written this book, like all of my other books, similar to when two old friends come together over a beer or a glass of wine, and to chew the fat or discuss each other's lives and problems. By reading a book we should have the opportunity to think about what message is being shared. This book is not, in essence, a "how-to" manual or even didactic in nature, but rather nudging you to look at life through perhaps someone else's eyes, and my own wish is that you have an open mind and heart when reading the suggestions within.

Take on-board those things that you find interesting and useful – and the rest you can throw overboard or keep for a later date. I also realise and accept that we already have enough people in our lives telling us what to do; when to do it; and how to do something - and my ultimate intent is not to add to the amount of stress in your life at this moment.

It should also be considered that this might not be the most ideal time to be reading this book. If that is the case, this book will be there waiting for you ... when you are ready. However, if you are open and willing to explore something new, have fun at the same time, and put into practice some of the ideas enclosed, then I am looking forward to having you come along with me for the ride.

A note for my Kindle (sample) readers. One significant advantage of reading this piece of work in an e-book format is that updates can be added or subtracted by the author, and this is what I intend doing here.

According to my editors, I do, nevertheless, frequently go off topic and on wild tangents. For this, I apologise. I do this, however, because I want to give "more" and get my readers to think "more" about other critical related issues and topics; and also, to qualify my statements or facts. Therefore, there are in this book a few external **hyperlinks**[1] to other interesting websites and articles.

And finally, to boot, I also write about the stuff that I personally find fascinating. So, I write about the stuff that I also want to read.

For this, I apologise in advance!

With love …

Antony xxx

PS: Each chapter heading is accompanied by a different colour. It is now more understood that the chameleon changes its colour according to its mood. Meaning that the brighter the colour – the increased tension or aggressive "mood" regarding the topic matter. The blander the colour – the more harmonious we might feel about the subject matter.

PPS: I have purposely used double-lined spacing between paragraphs - to slow the reading pace down a little. I want you to enjoy and relish these words and sentences, together with the messages behind them.

Breathe, smile and enjoy!

1

INTRODUCTION

"RED" - SHAME

"I hate having to do small talk. I'd rather talk about deep subjects. I'd rather talk about meditation, or the world, or the trees or animals, than small, inane, you know, banter." - Ellen DeGeneres

Have you ever looked back at some past event in your life and realised that, just by meeting that specific person, perhaps by chance, at a particular time, suddenly changed the whole course and direction of your life? It is these moments – that spice of life – which this book wishes to explain and even encourage. I want to argue that by using small talk, to strike up a conversation with someone, might just be enough to ignite these life-changing events.

You might be wondering what the reason is for having a colourful chameleon on the front cover of this book. The word "chameleon" derives from the Greek χαμαί (on the ground) and λέων (lion). These are just some of the unusual attributes of this little colour-changing lizard. And, as explained throughout this book, when we enter into a small talk situation we first need **the courage of a lion**[2]; plus we also need to be grounded, observant and even a little bit curious.

> *Antony:* Good morning, Elodie. Can you see and hear me okay?
> *Elodie:* Yes.
> *Antony:* How are you feeling today?
> *Elodie:* I'm fine ... and you?
> *Antony:* I'm also fine ... a little cold but that's okay. Tell me, Elodie, what's the weather like today in France?
> *Elodie:* It's a little cloudy and cold.
> *Antony:* The same here in Germany. By-the-way, what did you do at the weekend?
> *Elodie:* We had a relaxing weekend ... went for a small hike in the woods and afterwards just spent the rest of the time on our sofa watching tv.

This is a typical first conversation with one of my online students. When she arrives in the classroom, I – the teacher – need to take control of the situation – to "set the table", so to speak; to assess the teaching situation; and also, to prepare for the oncoming new lesson. These few sentences of small talk take but a few seconds to "catch-up"; making sure that everything is working well with the technology; and perhaps more importantly, her ability – as a student - to actively work with me once again.

Small talk, as a frequent topic, when teaching Business English over the years, has been something that I teach well; it is something that "flows" unlike English grammar; and, its importance

INTRODUCTION

should not be underestimated or ignored - especially in the business world.

Teaching this topic to my international students, I quickly came to realise that my own perception of the importance of small talk, was generally not accepted in some cases. In fact, most were somewhat hostile when the topic of small talk arose – together with the role-play exercises (which is only an elaborated form of practising small talk).

Why is it that some "seem" to have it easy when speaking to strangers and yet for others, this is more stressful and complicated than giving a presentation about advanced mathematics without notes or time to prepare? Also, this is even more stressful when we have to or need to small talk with someone in a language other than our mother tongue.

The primary tenet of this book is for me to ask you to consider three things:
  a) Firstly, to consider if you are willing to use small talk … more of the time?
  b) Are you willing to make your encounters with others less stressful by using small talk?
  c) And finally, could you be a tad more curious about your fellow human beings, in general?

In **Chapter Two** we examine what small talk is - and what it is not. We look at the different dictionary definitions, plus what it means to different people. Small talk highlights our uniqueness, especially when observing all modern and ancient human forms of communication. I will argue that it is preparational in nature and should not be ignored – mainly because we are social beings and as so we are just part of the sum totality of the whole – or society at large.

Chapter Three (one of the longer chapters) continues on from the previous chapter by looking at the importance of small talk in both our business and private lives; We might consider small talk as a game - despite having a certain amount of struggle involved; We will shed light on the helpful melody of the English language – which, inadvertently helps the continuation of a conversation and follows the beat of the heart.

Also examined in this chapter, is why it is essential to take control of a small talk interaction and one's own ultimate intention; Understanding the different levels of stress using the SSL – Stress Standardisation Level; Small talk takes courage, together with doing something special for someone else; How speech impediments add extra pressure when speaking and how feelings differ from facts; How our answers might be too short – perhaps appearing arrogant or rude; and how taking turns in a conversation; and how stressed words allow the other person to speak.

The uses of phatic expressions and how they might hinder "true" conversation; Talking about how we feel – the problem of feeling "fine"; How speaking about the weather can calm; Why we should not disguise our accents and dialects; and learning how native speakers use and pronounce the weak verbs and the schwa. And finally, how the millennials only really want to be included – which begs the point about our own prejudices

INTRODUCTION

regarding the young and their apparent disinterest.

Chapter Four considers the importance of the subject of trust before we might go into business with another; Through the small talk situation, we can build subtle trust from the first encounter – one stone at a time.

When we are needed to share information with someone else we must be authentic, as this trust is built up over time; and small talk can be an excellent way of making this happen naturally and without pressure.

We know that when someone makes us feel welcome – this is sometimes more important than price, delivery dates or the product or services being offered. When the client "feels" understood, secure and welcome when visiting a new company - and that all his personal needs are being fulfilled by the employee who – for example, pick him up from the airport and is friendly and professional while visiting the company – then going into business with this company is natural and more accessible.

Chapter Five examines the importance of body language communication. Even before we utter a word, our appearance - or first impressions - speak volumes; Why most strive and struggle to "fit into" the dominant society; What we wear and the attitudes and accepted norms of dress code; How the learning and practising of body language skills make small talk more manageable and allows flow; Why having good eye contact - perhaps with a slight smile - doesn't automatically mean being aggressive or threatening; and finally, the reason we can use touch to interrupt, relax and disempower the aggressive actions of others.

In **Chapter Six**, we look at the science of hearing our own name within a group – and how this makes us feel; A smile is sometimes too much – making way for a half smile or smirk; How an open hand can show others that we mean no harm; The business handshake should not prove dominance but rather to offer the other stability and respect – together with a good eye-to-eye contact.

In **Chapter Seven**, we discuss what is considered to be "good" and "bad" topics of having fruitful small talk conversations. This chapter is tinged with some basic universal laws and as so, might appear from the outset a little odd, but at the same time, strangely familiar and intuitively right; We examine finding the right frame of mind; perhaps a deeper reason for small talk; when to break the silence; when to avoid small talk; the different codes of speaking; vocabulary mirroring; open and closed-ended questions; truly listening before speaking; the three types of listening and empathy; echoing as a useful tool; using question tags to show that we are following; our self-disclosure list; the numbers game; flirting, speed dating and practising our elevator speech beforehand.

Chapter Eight compares small talk to any other essential business skills; it examines the advancement of telecommunication platforms and the ever-increasing struggle of modern optimisation; How our own language and culture can be seen as being ethnocentric; how describing nation states and cultures as being fleeting moments in time; how utterances rather than words can be meaningful (phatic expressions); the comparison between cultural awareness versus etiquette; the necessity of connectivity – especially with the young; how men and women communicate; and finally, how striving to be perfect and accepting to make a mistake or to err.

In the last chapter, **Chapter Nine**, we tie up loose ends and answer any other topics or discussions. We compare once again the traits of a chameleon to that of human interaction; accepting that some people do not want to use small talk; either we can quickly devour a gateau or enjoy it: the what-ifs; understanding more about the "why" in business; HR Departments needing to use small talk to see how agile someone is; how collegiality and teamwork are linked; not having to avoid social occasions; using "you" in English but still keeping a sentence formal and respectful.

A perfect example to illustrate the stress involved in instigating a small talk conversation can be seen here in this YouTube video from one of my favourite British journalists, John Harris, when he was interviewing people in **the UK about the fiasco which is/was Brexit**.[3] He says that asking people in the street about an interesting topic…

> *"... it is like jumping into a very cold swimming pool and not wanting to do it."*

That is precisely how most people feel when starting a small talk conversation. This is quite normal but, as you will find out later, well worth the time and the effort.

The French philosopher and novelist, Jean-Paul Sartre, in one of his books, **Huis Clos (No Exit)**,[4] explains the existentialist view that *"hell is other people"*. If you believe in this idea or you are not interested in examining the possible importance of small talk, then please do not buy and read this book.

If, however, you agree with me about its importance - or willing to take another look or even just are curious about the subject - then just sit back and enjoy reading this book ... and I hope to hear more about your own opinions regarding this matter at a later date.

We will, later on, be examining the important work of Geert Hofstede. In his work, he states that we must first be able to speak the language in order to achieve cultural awareness. For this reason, every time that I teach my non-native English-speaking students, I am, at the same time, facilitating in propagating tolerance and trying to break down any barriers of prejudice and hate for the other; and thus - as a teacher and trainer – doing my little something for harmony, world peace and social justice.

2

WHAT THE HELL IS SMALL TALK, ANYWAY?

"ORANGE" - *GRIEF*

*"I'm not good at meeting people, and
I'm not good at small talk."* - Nick Frost

Small talk, as a subject or topic for the businessman or woman, should definitely be highly regarded in the business world and even taught and treated like any other necessary "skill-set" or qualification – comparable with negotiating, rhetoric, time and change management, or perhaps even just basic presentation skills.

It is not only an important skill-set but might be best seen as preparational in nature, and as so, building the groundwork or foundation of the person speaking. It is similar to smelling the bouquet of a glass of fine wine before tasting; it might be likened to spending some extra time to set the table before your guests arrive; or even preparing the organic ingredients needed for an excellent meal before the cooking process even begins.

Before we look at some dictionary definitions, let us first discuss what small talk is **not**.

Small talk is not irrelevant, even in today's busy world. As explained later, it should never be seen as a "waste of time", regardless of the amount of time we have. It is certainly not trivial, petty or better than just remaining silent and alone in the corner of a room. This important type of conversation should never be deemed as boring, regardless of whether we think we have "more important" things to do. And these small talk conversations should never ever be judged as being "forgettable" or "forced".

The majority of my research, looking into the reasons why some people find small talk boring, tedious and forgettable, is just that they do not appear to "care" about other people in their environment.

For those, however, there will come a time when they realise that:

> *"... no man is an island."*

and our own independent existence in the world is and has always been reliant on other people. For example, these are the people who repair our motorways and roads; the postman delivering our letters; those hard-working waiters and waitresses serving us coffee; the pizza delivery guy on his moped; the shopkeepers; or the neighbour next door, who greets us each morning with a smile. More of this quote from John Donne later.

Once again, those that do not want to subscribe to this idea of being "an important part of the whole", generally end up ... alone, frustrated and bitter.

This is mainly because we, as human beings - and is uniquely integrated into our world and society - are all social beings; rather than being its opposite ... anti-social, alienated, ascetic, asocial, austere, cold, cynical, eremitic, hermit-like, introverted, misanthropic, reclusive, remote, reserved, retiring, solitary, standoffish, uncommunicative, unfriendly, unsociable and withdrawn – all of which have negative connotations in society as a whole.

The Cambridge Dictionary defines small talk as:

"... conversation about things that are not important, often between people who do not know each other well."

Collins Dictionary describes it as:

"... polite conversation about unimportant things that people make at social occasions."

And the Oxford English Dictionary offers:

"... polite conversation about unimportant or uncontroversial matters, especially as engaged in on social occasions."

However, my own definition is something that I want to discuss in this book. Small talk is ...

"... like a game of tennis; it is an excellent way of offering kindness and respect; it is a way of conversing with another in an open and non-threatening way. Unlike tennis, it is primarily preparational in nature and should not be seen as a fight or contest between individuals; however, it can build the foundations of trust; it offers friendship, warmth, caring, understanding and a mutual respect for some other person – and for no better reason than bestowing the hand of friendship to another - and being curious about someone else at the same time."

-**Coach Antony (2019)**

To follow more about **Small Talk** - '**Enlightening Interruptions**', please follow the hashtag:

#SmallTalkIs

#SmallTalkIs

Human communication is something which is taken for granted most of the time, but it has developed and evolved in us humans and is *sui generis* in nature; originating from the Latin: *of its own kind*. It is so complex that even when (socio)linguists and psychologists strive to explain the multitude of new ways of contacting and interacting with each other, we have to conclude – perhaps in awe - just how special and unique this skill really is.

Body language, too – the mimic, the gestures, the hand movements when speaking - are all part of communication and so failing or missing when we use symbols to express ourselves. The telephone … before the telephone was perhaps a telegram … before that a messenger (don't kill the messenger) and bells ringing, sirens wailing in a war, and before that, smoke or beacons of fire on distant hills.

-

Before we move onto the next chapter, let us recap some of the fundamental ideas discussed in this chapter.

- *- The use of small talk should be highly regarded and should be adopted as a skill-set.*
- *- Even if it takes time – we should still make time for entering into a small talk situation.*
- *- Ignore the opportunity of human interaction with others at your peril.*
- *- Small talk is just part of the uniqueness of social interaction and communication.*

Small talk is ... being an ambassador for your company and your country. Be proud to be kind!

3

WHY THEN, IS SMALL TALK SO HARD BUT IMPORTANT?

"YELLOW" - *FEAR*

"I am not a vivacious person in real. I hate smiling. I hate doing small talk." - Anushka Sharma

So, now we know somewhat more about what small talk is and is not, we can now discuss its importance; not only for the business person but also in our normal day-to-day lives. Moreover, if it really is so incredibly significant, then we must at the same time also examine why we "struggle" so much with understanding and accepting these facts; and perhaps consider why we do not use it more of the time?

Small talk might best be seen as a game … perhaps a friendly game of tennis or badminton. It should be seen as an interactive event between two or more people. Despite being a game, there is also an element of struggle in the activity. If we have ever played tennis with someone - perhaps a child - then we know that they struggle to hit the ball back over the net on a regular basis; there is little or no flow or fun; and both players end up feeling frustrated.

As mentioned before, small talk for me, at the start of a lesson, is like setting the table or preparing the ingredients for a meal. This is something that I do automatically now and something that I can also "use" in my private life – if and when I choose to do so.

It should also be remembered that each language has its own melody or rhythm. This is learned from childhood through primary interaction and listening. English speech has the following pattern:

de DUM | de DUM | de DUM | de DUM | de DUM

This rhythm or melody helps the continuation of the conversation – together with the tone and volume. Later on in this book, we will be discussing more about the advantages of having a small talk conversation when using the English language.

To illustrate its importance, let us examine once again the example given previously; a typical conversation between one of my students and myself at the start of a lesson. An excellent example of small talk in real life – setting the scene of a productive lesson. Yet... why spend so much time beforehand rather than starting the "learning" lesson directly?

WHY THEN, IS SMALL TALK SO HARD BUT IMPORTANT?

When I first start working with one of my one-to-one online students, I want to do several things - all packed into the first few minutes and, in my opinion, all incredibly important and necessary to have a successful lesson.

Let us look at each sentence once again and analyse what I am in fact doing:

1. Antony: *Good morning, Elodie. Can you see and hear me okay?*

These first two sentences - my opening gambit, if you like - is me presenting my intent; this is key and indicates how I want the lesson to progress. This sentence is also offering a positive first impression as the teacher, and also to take total control of the situation. For it is me ... wanting to give my students the best possible "lesson or session" in the allotted time. It also allows her to "acclimatise" to my voice; its melody; its accent or dialect; and rhythm of speech.

We have to remember that I do the majority of my teaching online now – which was something that I had no real intention of doing – as I prefer to be with the people I teach – there and present in the same room. Nonetheless, it has been most convenient because I cannot and do not want to travel to Lake Constance, Lyon, Vienna, Tokyo, Detroit or Ninjang province on a daily basis.

Strangely enough, this opening sentence – like when first instigating a conversation with someone - is quite likely the most stressful (see diagram below).

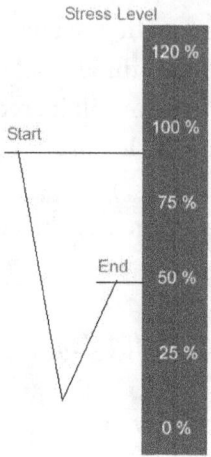

So basically there are a plethora of possible things that might go wrong and influence the teaching and learning experience. For example, I do not know if the technology is going to work; if the student is going to arrive (on time); and how the student is feeling – knowing if his or her ability to be able to comprehend what I am teaching that day.

In one of my previous books, I talked extensively about the SSL (Stress Standardisation Level), to explain the differing levels of stress at work … despite this, we can also use it here to examine the different forms of stress in our private and personal lives, but also when entering into a small talk conversation with someone else.

SSL
Stress Standardisation Level

- **Level Zero Stress:**
  (medium-level stress, boredom, short-term contracts)
  negative stress through inactivity, insecurity & exclusion.

- **Level One Stress:**
  (low-level, short-term stress)
  positive stress through challenges and variety.

- **Level Two Stress:**
  (high-level stress, long-term, negative stress)
  by having more to do than humanly possible.

- **Level Three Stress:**
  (extremely high-levels of stress, over a long-term
  negative and continuous stress resulting in
  burnout & mental/physical illness or disease.

Coach Antony 2019

Similarly, when approaching someone at a wedding or another occasion, such as welcoming a visitor to the company, to perhaps initiate a low-level conversation takes real courage. We are doing something new – bringing something unique into being – similar to an artisan.

When instigating small talk, we are doing something quite special for that person, plus at the same time, for our company. We should always remember that this social interaction should never be taken-for-granted – i.e. that we are speaking a language other than our own; that we are representing your company; and subtly highlighting the company's image and reputation at the same time.

For this reason, the first words out of your mouth matter, together with the volume and the tone of the words used. As discussed later, they should enhance an implicit mixture of friendliness and curiosity about the other.

***

I would, at this juncture, like to make a short interlude, regarding (dysgraphia, dyscalculia and dyslexia) impediments in general; together with those people who are affected by these afflictions; and how this might negatively influence them to use small talk, mainly because of the stress and frustration involved.

We have to remember that, if one has a problem speaking or reading something in a native language – then it would be self-obvious that that same person is going to have the same or similar issues when speaking a foreign language.

The academic research on **stuttering and stammering**[5] shows these disorders or disfluencies are put into one category - in my opinion, they are something entirely different and need some differentiation.

Stuttering:
Stuttering is a speech disorder, in which the spoken word is hindered by broken repetitions of the same word "… su … su… su… such", for example. The first letter or syllable is usually voiced, thereafter comes the struggle to complete the word and sentence in full.

Stammering:
Stammering, by contrast, there is an impediment to get even the first syllable out of the mouth. This usually happens with an involuntary silence – sometimes accompanied by a distorted

facial expression.

Both stammerers and stutterers experience significant stress and frustration when striving to communicate with others. David Ward, writing in 2006, "Stuttering and Cluttering: Frameworks for understanding treatment,"[6] highlights what he calls: "**internal factors**", such as lack of confidence, self esteem or inadequate language skills: together with – "**external factors,**" such as peer-group and time pressure, stressful speaking situations and perfectionism when speaking.

> *"... the severity of the disorder is seen as likely to increase when demands placed on the person's speech and language system exceed their capacity to deal with these pressures."*

So the stress or pressure of, not only speaking to other people, in a small talk situation - together with speaking in a foreign language, at the same time – is highly likely to affect one's ability to perform at these times. An excellent modern example of this age-old impediment can be seen in the film: **The King's Speech**[7] about the renown speech impediment of the King of England in the 20th century.

As mentioned before, each language has its own pace or rhythm. In English, this rhythm usually simulates the rhythm of the heart. An excellent example of this can be seen in a short quote from one of Shakespeare's plays:

SMALL TALK - ENLIGHTENING INTERRUPTIONS

but SOFT| what LIGHT | through YON | der WIN | dow BREAKS
de DUM | de DUM | de DUM | de DUM | de DUM

In this scene, Romeo uses the usual iambic pentameter (a line of verse with five words) - each making up one short (or unstressed) syllable, followed by one long (or stressed) syllable).

Now, it follows that if this pace is impaired, and when we cannot get a word out - owing to stress or a speech impediment - this cannot only cause even more stress and frustration on our emotional being but can also affect our own general well-being and will undoubtedly mitigate the flow of a small talk conversation.

On a personal note, as a child, I stuttered severely, and this previous speech disorder or impediment still returns to me today under high levels of stress. Looking back, being at school in the 1970s in the UK, I do not think they – the school - had the knowledge or practicalities in dealing with such maladies.

I still remember today having to read something out loud from a book in front of my teacher and the rest of the class – and not being able to get the words out of my mouth - stress, panic and trauma still return today when thinking about that time at school.

***

In the next part of the conversation, we will concentrate on feelings. Feelings are different from facts ... feelings are unique and should not be questioned. If someone is "feeling" sad, then obviously, we cannot tell that same person, that he or she is not sad. This is diametrically opposed to facts. The fact that we have not achieved an expected target on time. This is a fact and thereby quantifiable. This then is "real" … in the sense that we can measure it and measure if it is truthful or not.

So when I ask my students:

Antony: *How are you feeling today?*

Implicit in this open first question is how that person "feels". This has less to do with the facts or reality … being busy, in pain, relaxed, stressed, etc. and more to do with the emotion of the current circumstance that the student is finding herself in.

There is, presumably, a significant problem, when asking how someone feels … that being, that most would answer with either:

Student: *Fine!*

Perhaps closely followed by:

Student: *And you?*

As the majority of my French students live in different regions of France, where the standard reply to this question might be:

How do you feel today?
Comment allez-vous aujourd'hui?

together with the appropriate or standard answer:

And you?
Et Vous? or Et Tu?

Once again, intercultural differences play an important role here. When two people in France or Germany might reply with either:

Et Tu? or *Et Vous?* **OR** *Und Du?* or *Und Ihnen?*

… this short reply might be totally acceptable in the French or German languages, despite this, and certainly in the business world (but especially in the UK), the French *Et Tu* (although being stated in the informal mode) is just too short, abrupt - and even bordering on the impolite for someone in the UK.

We will be examining and covering cultural differences later in the book, but for now, let us acknowledge that what we say is automatic in most cases – and should not be taken-for-granted.

Once again there is usually is a stress or intonation on certain words: for example, in the word "you" in a reply or sentence … highlighting the fact that we are now passing the ball or baton on to the next person – and so, expecting an answer.

Moreover, answering a question with an answer … *and you?* – then adding a follow-up sentence straight after … *How are you feeling today?* - sounds less abrupt and friendlier – thus helping to continue the conversation in some subtle way.

By personalising the small talk sentence, and by adding that second part of the reply: *How are **you** feeling today?* this completes or rounds the sentence, making it more conversational, rather than just the standard response that we often hear and expect.

Generally, when answering a question with another question, we are not really listening; in most cases these questions are just irrelevant and unhelpful – unless one is a politician, trying to avoid answering an awkward question being posed.

2. Elodie: *I'm fine and you?*

That said, what does this sentence exactly mean … and how does it add "value" or "meaning" to the opening gambit or oncoming conversation or interaction? Most of the time … it does not! Which is a real shame …

Generally, when someone replies:

I am fine! **or** *I'm okay!*

This statement is similar to the previous example: How do you do? It is just something to say … without really meaning or asking anything. These are called **phatic expressions**[8] – though, for the purpose of starting a conversation, these types of sentences are mostly accepted.

We will be discussing phatic questions and expressions later on, for now, however, such as: *"How's it going?"* Is not really a question at all. The normal response is … *"Everything's fine."*

Very similar to: *"How do **you** do?"* replying ... *"... and how do you do?"* ... just phatic expressions.

When starting a lesson with a new student or client, I generally ask them to be honest with me. Honesty builds trust. I have a slide ready which shows someone wearing a t-shirt ... on the t-shirt are the words:

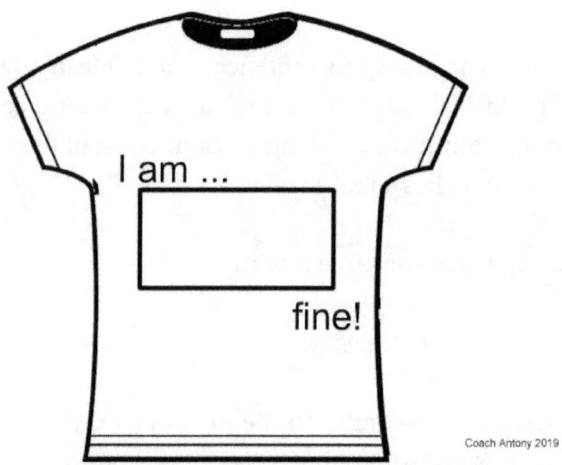

"I'm fine!" ... when some days we feel ... less than fine!

Some days we say that we are fine … when really we want to say:

"I am sad, depressed, stressed, hurt, ill, happy, overworked."

Being honest with the other is vital for several reasons. Firstly, as a teacher, I need to know how to proceed with that person on that particular day. I also need to know if the student is ill, tired, stressed or just generally feeling under the weather. I then know 'more' - helping me to adjust the oncoming lesson accordingly – together with their (in)ability to listen and learn.

There is now a strange case for not generally telling the truth especially in politics but also about how we are feeling – mainly due to it not being 'appropriate' in our professional lives. And certainly in the small talk arena, although this might be "true", talking about illnesses or states of emotions this might now not be suitable, welcomed or expected.

This goes both ways ... if I am feeling tired or under the weather, I normally like to share this with my students and clients. I am but a mere human ... living in the real world ... and, as so, fallible and sometimes even vulnerable.

>   **3. Antony:** *I'm also fine ... a little cold but that's okay. Tell me, Elodie, what's the weather like today in France?*

"**The weather?**" I hear you holler, rolling your eyes in disbelief, "... *how banal ... trite ... predictable and trivial form of small talk.*"

Still, in these few words, I allow my student to adjust or acclimatise to my own mood, my accent, my London dialect (tinged with having lived and worked in Germany for half my life), plus making sure that the technology (of working online with my students) is all working well and to an optimal level.

>   **4. Antony:** *The same here in Germany. By-the-way, what did you do at the weekend?*

>   **5. Elodie:** *We had a relaxing weekend ... went for a small hike in the woods and spent most of the time on the sofa.*

Extending the typical teacher/student connection, we move into something more personal and private. A short exchange of something outside the normal realm of teaching; something more profound and built up over several of previous lessons.

This "something extra", shows trust and an ongoing relationship. It is this give and take; this sharing - that is the icing on the cake; the salt on an egg; or even the sugar on strawberries.

We must also not forget that speaking to someone in a foreign language means that we have to deal with not being understood by the words we speak, but also because of any dialects or accents that the person might possess.

For example, if we are speaking English to a German person, we might not understand the Bavarian accent; similarly, if we talk to someone who lives in Brest, in France, they will talk differently than someone who lives in Dijon or Marseilles.

We should be proud of our **accents and even dialects**[9]. These characteristics make up who we are. Strive not to cover-up or disguise our unique way of speaking or use another supposedly "better" accent to impress others. Even if we do, other people can generally "feel" that something is 'not right' or of the speaker trying to hide something.

Similarly, if we come from a country – whose first language is not English – we also have to deal with something called: "**weak forms**[10]" of words. These are syllable sounds that become unstressed in connected speech and are often then pronounced as a **schwa**[11]. For example, in the sentence below the first '**do**' is a weak form and the second '**do**' is stressed.

*What **do** you want to **do** this evening?*

Similar to this might also be the words: **been, for, to** and **you!**

been /bn/ Have you *been* here long? **bin**
for /f/ It's a present *for* my dad. **fer**
to /t/ Are you going *to* the party tonight? **ter**
you /j/ /ju/ Do *you* like chocolate? Du-ya-lik – **ya**

All of these stresses make small talk conversation much harder for the non-English speaking person who is trying to use small talk on holiday or as part of his or her professional life.

The rest of this book deals with and examines just how small talk is necessary and, in my opinion, thoroughly important and useful.

Nevertheless, we must also remember, and perhaps accept, that not everyone may be capable of "enjoying" having a small talk conversation; regardless if we do this in our professional or private lives.

And for the millennials – those who perhaps do not really understand what it was like before the freedom of digitalised communication – they still have the reputation of what I will call: "general avoidance". Despite demonstrating a heightened disconnection to the outside world for most of the time … by donning on headphones and earbuds; having a continual downward glance at their hand-held devices; and thus avoiding direct eye contact – the young still yearn at a deeper level to be just "accepted" and allowed to gain entry into the main hierarchical society.

Before moving on to the next chapter, where we will be discussing the relationship between trust and small talk, let us recap some of the important ideas presented in this chapter.

- *- Small talk might best be seen as a game that we all play – or decide not to play*
- *- Each language has its own melody*
- *- Using small talk to assess the situation and showing intent*
- *- Acclimatising to our accents and dialects*
- *- Calming the situation – controlling possible stress, asking non-threatening small talk questions*
- *- Doing something new – bringing something unique and special into being for that person*
- *- Speech impediments causing small talk difficulties and tension in the native language*
- *- Feelings are different from facts*
- *- The stressed words – helping to continue the conversation*
- *- How we (mis)use phatic expressions – although this does not really help the continuation of a conversation*
- *- Being honest and sincere with the other*
- *- How sharing builds trust and adds flavour to a relationship*
- *- Being proud of our accents and dialects*
- *- How some words in sentences sound different – the schwa*

SMALL TALK - ENLIGHTENING INTERRUPTIONS

Small talk is ... linked with success and happiness, and something which takes less energy to carry out rather than trying to avoid it!

4

BUILDING TRUST & SHARING PERSONAL INFORMATION

"GREEN" - *ANGER*

"That's all small talk is - a quick way to connect on a human level - which is why it is by no means as irrelevant as the people who are bad at it insist. In short, it's worth making the effort." - Lynn Coady

When we enter into a small talk interaction with someone else – we are typically required, needed or expected to share something personal. Something from our lives that we are willing to share with a stranger (see Chapter Six - Self-Disclosure List). Naturally, we could always lie or exaggerate the truth ... but as mentioned earlier, every time that we lie or not tell the whole truth, we are required to remember that specific lie ... because we might need it again for future reference.

When we meet someone for the first time, I believe it is essential to first be authentic and sincere, but more importantly ...

truthful. For every untruth we tell ... we are putting at risk, not only the new relationship but also our own reputation or integrity - which we are building the foundation of, at that same initial moment.

Everyone has secrets or perhaps something that we might want to keep under wraps – something small; large; or possibly something more damaging. When we share little parts of ourselves, those small things that make up our unique and original selves – this sharing is the spice of life and something that we can use to make good and interesting conversation with someone else.

Like meeting a possible new friend at a party ... we give them or tell them something small and see what they do with this information. Do they use this nugget against us at a later date or do they keep it confidential and secret? Therein lies the foundation of what being a "good" friend is.

Before going into a private or business relationship, we must first build up a certain amount of trust. Once this trust is achieved, we can then decide to share something 'more'; something intense or intimate or even something personal. This sharing might be seen as an exchange – extending the relationship and making it stronger and more developed.

We are not likely to go into business with a person or company which we do not honestly believe in or trust – we have a funny feeling about that person. Though sometimes we are asked to greet visitors to our company or perhaps meet someone new, and it is our job to make them feel welcome – as seen when picking up a client or customer from the airport or train station.

It is a way, for me as a writer, and for you as a person in the business world, to explore something different and perhaps novel; because it is this difference ... it is this spice of life ... which makes the difference between just existing in the world and that of truly enjoying the entire process and relishing in something new, exciting and unique.

The word "curiosity" is key here! Rather than curiosity killing the cat, we might believe it to be an integral part of our human DNA and, more importantly, perhaps a gift ... like the gift that was given to **Pandora**[12]; or for us to communicate "better" with our fellow human beings.

One significant advantage of being human is that we have the ability and opportunity to learn from everyone we meet – something that the writer Stendhal used as a research method in most of his writings, but specifically when writing about the human condition.

We must never forget that when we take the plunge and talk to someone – perhaps a stranger – we are in fact doing them a favour and not the other way around! This is something which I repeat to my students learning Business English ... we are doing them a favour by speaking a foreign language or making light conversation when meeting and chatting to someone for the first time. And please also remember, that small talk is even harder in a foreign language, because of the possible mispronunciations, erroneous meanings and definitions of certain similar looking words – false friends.

We should, nonetheless, never forget that, when someone does not want to speak with us … that has to be fine too. Once again … we can only do our best at any one point in time. Indeed, we can learn from the mistakes that we make and hopefully not make the same or similar mistakes again in the future.

> *"Insanity is repeating the same mistakes and expecting different results."* - Narcotics Anonymous (1981)

This has been something that is all part and parcel of living in a world where sometimes our private information is "shared" either knowingly or without our consent. This can be seen in the **Facebook/Cambridge Analytica**[13], known now to be the most significant data breach ever – targeting the Brexit voters and positively affecting the Brexit campaign referendum in the UK in 2016; but also to predict and influence the choices at the ballot boxes in the US – and favouring Donald Trump and his campaign.

In conclusion, and before we move onto other topics, please remember that when we meet someone and start to talk with them about ourselves, we are "trusting" that person with information which might not be generally known. This information may not be freely available – which brings into question the idea of **data harvesting** [13a] and/or data protection. We can read more about the do's and don'ts in Chapter Six.

But, more importantly now, we should not be paranoid about this subject – just be sensible and have due diligence when sharing information either in person or online.

-

Before we move onto the next chapter, let us recap some of the important ideas discussed in this chapter.

- *- We are needed or expected to share some information with others*
- *- Telling the truth and being authentic/sincere*
- *- Sharing is the spice of life*
- *- Exchanging small nuggets of information and seeing what happens*
- *- Trust is built using an ongoing exchange of information*
- *- Curiosity is a part of our DNA*
- *- Learning from everyone we might meet*
- *- We are doing them a favour – when speaking to someone – especially clients or customers*
- *- Accepting that when someone is not interested in small talk*
- *- The problem with data harvesting and data protection in the modern world*
- *- Be sensible and show due diligence when sharing information online and with others*

SMALL TALK - ENLIGHTENING INTERRUPTIONS

Small talk is ... allowing for those special interactions to lead to something new and exciting!

5

DRESS CODE, EYE CONTACT & THE POWER OF TOUCH

"BLUE" - *NEUTRALITY*

*"But each day, when she walks to the sea
She looks straight ahead, not at me."* - The Girl from Ipanema

So that we feel confident or more confident, most might think and feel that they have to "look the part". Without wanting to appear stiff, dull or conservative, most will agree that we feel better when we look better. This inevitably follows that when we feel better – our ability to converse more easily with someone – perhaps in a small talk conversation – is somewhat more natural.

The majority just want to fit in; blend in; or adapt into the dominant culture or the groups within our society. Although some may wish to be unseen or not noticed, others want to be different and unique, either being extravagant or non-conventional - perhaps because they want to show creativity and diversity – and residing outside-the-box, is sometimes more important than towing the line and following the conventional and expected norms and values.

Although the following video more than likely is a spoof, it is still interesting to watch – analogically speaking - how we as humans might adapt to our environment (better) – perhaps having the ability to camouflage and readily adapt:

Chameleon Changing Color[14]
https://youtu.be/ioblgpA5eTo

As mentioned previously, we must adapt to our surroundings – and being a great small talker – makes this interaction easier and overall less stressful most of the time.

We, as humans, do not want to be seen or treated as an outcast – mainly because this "fitting in" and being accepted has to do with our own existence within the society, as seen in Maslow's hierarchy of needs. At the bottom of Maslow's triangle are the physiological needs of a person – the basics for human survival – water, food and shelter.

In the following YouTube video, we can examine how a homeless man is treated by the public:

"They Put A Homeless Man In A Suit And He Asks For Money On The Streets" [15]

This highlights the importance of appearance and our willingness to either help others in apparent need - or not.

This homeless man politely asks for money for some time, and not one person is willing to assist him ... many hardly even acknowledge his presence or being.

Later, this same homeless person is then smartened-up; he has his beard and hair trimmed and is given some better, cleaner clothes to wear. He is then given a mobile phone and stands in the same place as before.

This same man has suddenly "changed", because when he now asks strangers for money – perhaps for a coffee or a subway ticket home - people are now incredibly generous, giving him far more than what he was actually asking for. Why is this? What has happened?

We could ask ourselves these questions. Is it because we considered "all" homeless people as outcasts? Has our view of these people become subtly conditioned or changed over time? Or do we just assume now that "all" homeless people are just asking for money - either because they want to buy alcohol or drugs? Or, and something which has become more popular recently, that they do not actually "need" the money because they are professional beggars and, as so, not "needy" at all?

So, even before an utterance of small talk, we are, in fact, unconsciously speaking volumes by what we wear and the gestures we make. Regardless of our opinion regarding small talk, most will agree that our appearance - or the personal image that we want to project to the outer world - is paramount. This representation of how we want to be seen and judged, indicates how we firstly feel about ourselves, and then perhaps secondly our current mood or state of mind.

Even if we have little or no money, try to ensure that we have clean, "nice" clothes … spend some time on our hair (and beard or make-up). This first image or impression is the most important thing that we can do – in both our private and business lives. Good make-up generally makes us feel great and certainly more confident. However, not too much, otherwise it looks like we are hiding something … something that the person will want to inquire about.

A client of mine would meet up with the same customer at least three or four times before she carried out the actual service which she offered. She would write down what she wore the last time she met them … so that she didn't wear the same clothes twice. Women seem to appreciate this planning generally more than men. Men usually just wear trousers/pants, a jacket and a shirt … alternating perhaps with a different coloured tie or shirt for some variations of a theme.

Living in a large city there is a general tendency to always avoid eye contact, especially at close range; meaning that from a "safe" distance we observe the person who is walking towards us. This is called **civil inattention**.[17]

When that same person gets to about 2 or 3 metres from ourselves, we either look straight ahead or down at the floor – thus avoiding potential conflict or confrontation; meaning that if we want to appear self-confident or friendly, we need to "be seen" beforehand, and at this "safe" distance.

As mentioned previously, we observe or take-in information about someone else in our vicinity – long before we actually get close to them. The way they are walking … slow and unsure or head upright with a bounce of self-confidence in their stride.

Also, if we think of a depressed or sad person walking along a street, we know or can imagine the following:

- … about his or her head being lowered looking down
- … their pace is slow and erratic

Now think about a positive, happy person walking along a street, we imagine the following:

- … he or she is walking confidently
- … head held high and perhaps having a smile.
- … a definite stride or even a swagger

As mentioned previously, in most countries physical contact with those we do not know is prohibited – even more so, when we are talking about men-men contact.

Moreover, the handshake is, for the most part, accepted – except perhaps in some Muslim countries, where a male should not touch a female – even in a handshake.

The **French**[17] and **Russian**[18] population sometimes use a kiss on the cheek or *Faire la bise* when greeting colleagues or friends. So, each country and nationality make differing "rules" to follow – which can cause problems to a visitor or someone from outside the culture.

Although the kissing on the cheek is not widely used in the UK or in Ireland, it does happen. Hugging is something entirely different, especially in the US. And strangely enough, the French only have a word for cuddling and not hugging - *se caliner* to cuddle - and not to hug or embrace.

Before we move onto the next chapter, let us briefly recap about some of the critical issues discussed in this chapter.

- *- How using the correct dress code – helps in the small talking situation.*
- *- How we want to be seen and judged*
- *- First impressions are really important*

6

NAME CALLING, THE SMILE & AN OPEN HAND

"PURPLE" - *WILLINGNESS*

"A person's name is to that person, the sweetest, most important sound in any language." - Dale Carnegie

This quote from Dale Carnegie questions: what's in a name? Similarly, the **cocktail party effect**[19] highlights the importance of using someone's name correctly in a small talk conversation; and at the same time, making them feel "important" and restating and confirming out loud that they actually exist in the world.

When we hear our own name being used or spoken in company … this unconsciously reinstates or confirms our own existence … it brings us into the now, like being on the *qui vive*: "being in a state of heightened vigilance."

On the contrary, ignoring someone or getting someone's name

wrong - either in its entirety; its pronunciation; or even in the spelling we use – this may mean that the person speaking has little or no respect for that person being addressed.

The importance of a smile. A natural smile from a baby or young child is very contagious. Yet, as we mature we increasingly associate people who smile at us either as a "come on" or possibly that they are just a little bit crazy. So, the smile that we wear has to be the right kind of smile. Anyhow, a **smirk**[20] is something similar to a smile but more like a half-smile ... not corny or even intimidating but more authentic and something that many actors and celebrities choose to use.

When approaching someone, especially in the business arena, we usually approach, smile and then offer an open hand; but have we ever asked ourselves ... why? Why on the Pioneer 10 and 11 deep space probes did they attach a plaque of two humans with the man showing an open hand?

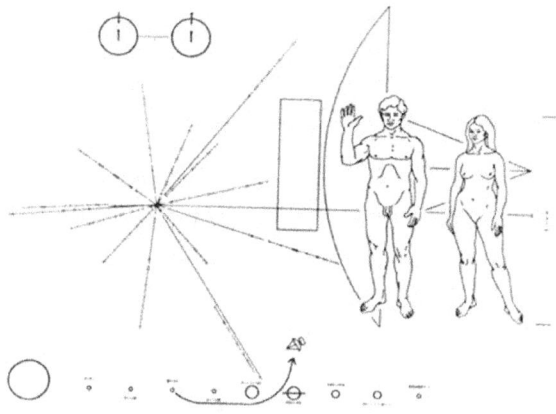

There is something instinctual or prehistoric when we see an open hand being offered to us. And the opposite is true... when we see someone with a clenched fist – our associations are of something or someone being threatening or even dangerous.

Similar to a warm smile, an open hand is usually perceived as being somewhat welcoming and shows the person who we are approaching that we are not carrying any dangerous weapons; and because of this, we also instinctively feel that that person is being non-violent and perhaps even friendly.

The strength or weakness of a **handshake**[21] can also indicate forcefulness or power "over" someone else. Yet, it can also show a certain amount of respect, balance and equilibrium all at the same time.

The two people who are shaking hands are not only making non-threatening bodily contact, but they are also making close-proximity eye-to-eye contact, as well. At the same time, they are mutually steadying each other; allowing both to hopefully find an equal and helpful steadfastness or footing.

All this helps to show assistance or a willingness to assist each other and even offer support – perhaps laying the foundations of a business relationship or friendship for the future.

Illustrated in:

"the 29-second handshake between President Macron and Donald Trump"[22]

In France, this was an obvious power-play rouse; it was more about vying for a position of dominance; had little or nothing to do with two world leaders meeting on a level playing ground; and certainly not two very different heads of state meeting on a diplomatic or friendly basis.

When we feel the warmth of another's hand in our own there is a long-forgotten rightness; perhaps taking us back to those childhood memories or a place of security enabled by siblings and/or parents. The handshake grants permission for same-sex touching in modern society, but still not permissible or accepted in some countries - especially where personal space is limited or highly regarded.

***

To illustrate the power of touch, I once remember being on a local bus in Greece, the bus driver returned my change for the just purchased ticket, with an old banknote plus several foreign coins. Still, this handful of unfamiliar currency was carefully deposited into the palm of my hand; with such determinism and apparent caring - like the touch of a friend's hand.

I did, nevertheless, notice later after taking my seat, that the driver had not given me the correct change ... far from it, to be honest. Although this was not a great deal of money, I let it go (being on holiday) and continued to watch this repeated interaction between the local bus driver and other boarding foreign passengers. What was really interesting, and something that I never forgot, was that the driver gave the people who followed me onto the bus, a smile and the same strange - touching of hands - to return their change – and, most likely, short-changing each of them in the process.

✳✳✳

We can also use touch to stop someone from speaking. We talked about saying someone's name out loud – making them stop to revel in their own existence. The same can be used or is true with a light touch on the top of someone else's hand or forearm.

-

Before we continue, let us go over some of the critical ideas talked about in this chapter.

- *- Using someone's name can be something very positive – making them feel "real"*

- *- Sometimes a half-smile or smirk serves to illustrate a thoughtful self-assuredness*
- *- An open hand generally indicates a non-threatening stance*

7

THE GOOD, THE BAD & THE UGLY TOPICS

"BROWN" - *REASON*

"I haven't got the patience for small talk, although I once saw a woman standing on her own in the corner, and I realised it was Monica Lewinsky, and I had the nicest evening with her – she was charming." - Sandi Toksvig

Later on in the chapter, we will be looking at a list that we are willing to speak to someone about – or not. But for now, let us concentrate on having the right frame of mind.

As indicated in previous chapters, we need to have a certain amount of courage before entering into a small talk situation. Remember too, that the whole idea of small talk is because we are basically nothing more than curious human beings. On top of this, this one interaction might possibly lead down some unknown paths; or even finding and unlocking hitherto unknown doors; and using keys, that have been in our possession for many years, but we never really realised their purpose before this journey and encounter.

Similar to **Breaking the Fast** when we wake up in the morning we have – **BreakFast**. When we speak to someone we **Break-Silence** – we are **Breaking the Silence** – but before we do, we need to do a certain amount of introspection, to see if we are in the right frame of mind - or not.

So, if we are angry, tired, sad, depressed, stressed or feeling other such negative emotions, then perhaps we should avoid speaking to others if possible – unless we are being forced into a small talk situation.

Our emotions and feelings radiate out from us like a beacon – communicating either a positive or negative beam of light; warning others of dangerous rocks, coastal hazards and stormy headlands ahead.

BBC Radio 4 Shipping Forecast 09/04/2014
https://youtu.be/mSq4nfH4y6Q?t=168[23]

However, sometimes we are forced to deal with other people. Chances are, this is not going to go well, because even without saying anything, your negative vibrations radiate out from you. Similarly to when we are speaking to someone we do not like … the form of things around that person are negatively charged and most can pick-up on this energy.

On the other hand, if one is neutral or positive this can prove to be something enlightening – if given a chance, as seen in this wonderful example of introducing oneself to someone we do not know, in the British mini television series about the family Durrell on the island of Corfu in the 1930s:

The Durrells in Corfu, Season 2: Episode 1 Scene[24]

As described in the video above, the best and easiest way to get into a conversation with someone else might be a short (but positive) and uncomplicated statement - generally followed by a question - perhaps relating to the previous statement or the circumstances in which we both find ourselves in. To make a conversation about something that that person has – for example, and dog or tie – and then comment on this - perhaps with a smile.

Imagine being at a wedding on your own. We do not know many people, but we see someone, and we wish to communicate with that person. As mentioned before, we are - at our root - social animals, and because of this, we are social via verbal and body communication.

Before we examine vocabulary mirroring, let us first examine the codes we use when speaking to someone. **Littlejohn**[25] (2002), agrees with **Bernstein**[26] in 1971 – stating that the 'code' a person uses symbolises their own social identity and perhaps even their class:

" ... people learn their place in the world by virtue of the language codes they employ".

Littlejohn goes on and uses the word "code" meaning to:

"refers to a set of organizing principles behind the language employed by members of a social group."

There are two types of codes when people talk to each other: **Elaborated Code and Restricted Code.** [27]

Restricted code is generally used by insiders - those who share ideas and knowledge about a topic or specific field or area. It is vibrant and flowery but quite concise at the same time. An eavesdropper would have significant problems following what was being said, just by listening in on the conversation.

The **Elaborated code**, on the other hand, needs no prior or shared understanding of a circumstance, nor for that matter, any specific knowledge about a topic or theme. Everything must be presented by explaining a new concept or idea, as the two people speaking, have possibly nothing in common. This particular code can be understood by anyone listening in – and for this reason, it is great when we want to enter into a conversation with someone who we presently do not know.

This book does not claim to have many hidden secrets, despite this, finding and using the "appropriate" level of **vocabulary mirroring,** considerably increases your chances of succeeding in a normal small talk situation. So, this vocabulary mirroring basically means finding the "right" level or tier of vocabulary when starting off a conversation with a stranger or someone that we do not know very well.

Below are listed the three levels of vocabulary mirroring plus several examples. **Level 1:** Easy words. **Level 2:** Easy words plus more adjectives. **Level 3:** Complicated and more descriptive words (specialist terminology or specific subjects or disciplines).

When we first meet someone – our goal is to meet that person at the same or a similar level. So, if he or she uses a basic word, such as: "work", we would also continue the conversation keeping it at that level. Similarly, if he or she uses the word: "profession" or "career" … we know that is higher up in the hierarchy of words, and so we should continue this conversation at that higher level.

For example, if we are an accountant, at an accountant's trade fair, then generally we do not need to use basic vocabulary to start and continue a conversation; mainly because they know the highly specified words and phrases known by most accountants or people who work in the Finance Department. This can then lead to a better social connectedness between speakers – see echoing below.

Finding and mirroring the level of the person you are small talking with.

LEVEL 3 — **Level 3** words are those words which are used in restricted code - the way two architects would converse with each other - subject specific.
convivial, lugubrious, verbalize, febrile or frigid.

LEVEL 2 — **Level 2** words are those words which are usually used in the written word. These words are more explanatonary in context.
jubliant, melancholy, utter, sweltering or chilled

LEVEL 1 — **Level 1** words are those everyday words that we use in normal speech. These words are learned via conversations from the past.
These are common words that most understand without explaination: happy, sad, speak, hot or cold.

Finding and using this right level of vocabulary can also lead to a lessening of social distance – while at the same time, increasing the feeling of safety and security, someone's likeability and even social cohesion.

There are two types of questions that we can ask: the first are **open-ended questions**[28] ... those that do not encourage a "yes" or "no" reply, for example:
"Tell me more about your recent holiday in Tuscany?"
"How do you see the future of Brexit?"
"What do you think about children watching commercials on tv?"
"What do you mean when you say: "better"?

The second type of question are those **closed-ended questions** [29] ... such as:

"Do you eat pizza?"
"Do you come here often?"
"Do you know the bride?"

Whenever possible, use an opened-ended question or statement. This takes the pressure off of you. However, we do not want the person to cringe by using corny first-liners, such as:

"Well, here I am! What now?"
"I think I've seen your face before."

When using statements about topical issues, we can ask if that person agrees or disagrees with us:

"What is your opinion about climate change?"
"Life is about getting up after a bad storm and being resilient. Do you agree?"

The best might be using observation and then following up with a question, such as:

"I went biking last week. Naturally, as to be expected, it rained cats and dogs for most of the day. Was your week any better?"

These types of statements and follow-up questions show friendliness, share vulnerability and show an interest in someone else.

Complimenting someone sincerely is generally a safe bet, unless they are having a really bad hair day. If this is the case, then please do not mention their hair. Find something authentic and honest to complement – otherwise talk about something else.

Remember that we should not use small talk to just fill the silence of a moment. Sometimes, silence is more important – but especially in other countries and cultures. Many times, it also shows that we are considering what someone else might have just said – and needing a respite to find a suitable answer or reply.

Also, before replying to a posed question, it might be respectful to pause very briefly … before answering (see the Scandinavian countries later). Also, really listen to the end of someone sentence. Quite often, we do not truly listen to the end of someone's sentence, because we are so passionate and/or eager about replying.

Do not hog the limelight … try not to boast or even show-off – this can be very annoying and can even end a conversation abruptly. Also, be aware of the time that we are talking … this should not be a one-man show but rather a shared interaction between two equals – a sharing of thoughts using words.

Active listening[30], sometimes used in therapy or counselling, is something that can be used in small talk. It allows for the opportunity to **really listen** to what someone has said; then respond. After that, we also need to have the ability to recall what has just been said, perhaps for a later date.

Reflective Listening[31] is listening and repeating back to the speaker what he or she has just heard – confirming the comprehension of all parties present. By using this method, we mitigate a potential problem of misunderstanding later in the conversation – it also shows underlying respect.

Empathetic listening[32] takes time to "really understand" the person who is speaking. It offers an opportunity for emotions to be shared ... before talking about any relevant facts. Empathetic listening should be non-judgemental in nature, rather than finding a solution for a specific problem.

Being empathic to the person we are talking to, unlike active listening, is a trait and something that we cannot learn or master – generally, either we are empathetic or not.

There are three basic types of empathy: **Affective or emotional empathy** (the ability to correctly react emotionally to someone else's mental state); **Cognitive empathy** (the ability to really comprehend or understand someone else's ideas and thought patterns); and **Somatic empathy** (is the ability to "feel" the physical pain experienced by another).

All the aforementioned listening techniques need to be mastered – mainly through the processes of practice and having a lot of patience, and all offer something special and unique. The better we can actively listen, reflectively listen and empathetically listen ... the more relaxed and enjoyable any future small talk conversations will be.

There should also be a certain 'momentum' when speaking

with someone. As mentioned before, imagine playing a game of tennis with a child or someone who cannot perform well, and your opponent does not return your serve … ever. How would that feel? Nevertheless, once we have returned the ball to each other a few times, the level of tennis and the enjoyment can then increase – as too, allowing for the level of complexity of the conversation or the game at hand.

By using echoing as a technique – repeating back to someone, what they have just uttered – is something that can be a useful tool in small talk; let them know that what they have just said has been heard, also that we are interested in something they just said – this could be either a name or a statement. This can also be an excellent way of better social interaction and closeness.

My name is Mary.
Mary? My mother's name was Mary.

I love abseiling.
Abseiling? Now, that is something that I always wanted to do. Tell me more?

Echoing can also be used when speaking to someone who perhaps has an unfamiliar dialect or when we do not "catch" or understand what the person has said – but wanting to remain friendly and respectful:

I called my c$$%& this morning.
Sorry … you called who … this morning?

My colleague. I called my colleague this morning.

We can also use echoing to relay that we are surprised at what someone has said:
*I won €200,000 in the lottery.
You won, how much?*

However, do not try to use echoing too much otherwise we might sound inauthentic or like a mynah bird.

We use question tags (also known as question tails) at the end of sentences to check information about someone or something. In small talk, this is great to continue a conversation and to show interest at the same time.

These are generally short questions that we put on the end of sentences, but particularly in spoken English to show that we are listening intently.

In a similar fashion, and just to make things more complicated, if the main part of the sentence is positive ... *She is a dentist,* - the question tag is negative – *isn't she?*

Similarly, if the main part of the sentence is in the negative form ... *You haven't been to London,* - the question tag is positive – *have you?*

People will do a variety of things when they do not want to engage in small talk; be that with neighbours, colleagues, or just strangers when out shopping. A younger person might just wear headphones to indicate this. Older people might just avoid eye contact or look down at the pavement. And perhaps we should just respect their wishes and let them be, rather than getting annoyed or frustrated.

Now, consider the topics that we are willing and unwilling to share with strangers in a small talk situation. This, once again, is preparational in nature and save struggle and stress when meeting someone for the first time – similar to the elevator speech – mentioned later on in this chapter. Despite this, it is essential to know what exactly we are personally willing to disclose or not.

The Self-Disclosure "Yes or No" List:

YES:
Name
Age
Nationality
Where we live?
Who we work for?
Married? Single? Separated? Divorced? Widowed?
Partner's name
Children
Holidays
Hobbies

NO:
Salary
Sexual Orientation

Political Views
Religious Affiliations
Weight
Health
Politics

When we disclose something about ourselves, we are being vulnerable ...

> *"We tend to meet disclosure with disclosure, even with strangers."*[33]

Being shy or introverted is generally regarded as the main reason why most do not embark into the art of small talk; for it is an "art" ... because this is something that we all often need to practice.

If we play the numbers game ... on average 95% of the time, we are going to be pleasantly surprised by the outcome of speaking to someone. For the other 5% - where people are non-responsive to your small talk instigations – we can first learn from this experience; and secondly, more than not, this has less to do with ourselves and more to do with how the other person is feeling at that particular moment in time.

Although it is certainly possible to "learn" to do something - or be something that we are not - we should remember Audrey Hepburn, as Eliza Doolittle in **"My Fair Lady"**[34], and DiCaprio, in **"Catch Me If You Can**[35]**"** – being that: *you can't fool all of* *the people all of the time ...* And nor should we want to. Respect and authenticity are important.

So, as mentioned above, we need to practice this interaction. There are certain similarities between **speed dating**[36] and social small talk. Both are generally fleeting moments of interaction. We are totally responsible for what we say or share – also important is our appearance. For we only have one chance to make a good first impression.

There is also a subtle line between **flirting**[37] and small talk. Both are generally complimentary, albeit the body language used - especially the eye contact – differs slightly. There might be more touching and smiling happening when flirting – although this also differs in other cultures. The best advice if we are unsure of something, is to ask:

Are you interested in what I do ...
or are you more interested in getting to know me better?

We are often nervous when we are stepping outside of our comfort zone. This might be the reddening of the face or throat. This is totally normal and, especially at the beginning, should be expected. Breathing, smiling and consciously lowering the shoulders might alleviate this nervousness.

Before completing this chapter, it is generally a good idea to practise our opening gambit by using something called the **Elevator Speech**.[39] These are a few rehearsed sentences that we can roll off our tongues when either talking about our company or ourselves – a verbal résumé or CV. By practising this more, but especially in stressful situations, i.e., picking-up some VIP from the airport and entering into conversation with him or her, makes explaining who we are much easier – the way a competent actor might learn his or her lines.

-

Before we talk about being culturally aware in the next chapter, let us examine a few of the main topics discussed in this chapter.

- - Finding the right frame of mind
- - A deeper reason for small talk – keys and locks
- - When to break the silence – BreakSilence
- - When to avoid small talk conversations
- - The different codes of speaking – elaborated and restricted
- - Vocabulary Mirroring – finding the right level
- - Open and Closed-ended questions
- - Listening to the complete sentence before speaking
- - Three types of listening – Active, Reflective and Empathic listening
- - Three types of empathy – Affective, Cognitive and Somatic empathy
- - How echoing can be a useful tool – and can increase social interaction
- - Respecting the non-communicative small talker
- - The Self-Disclosure List – Yes/No
- - 95% pleasantly surprised to be spoken too
- - The similarities between flirting and speed dating
- - Practising our Elevator Speech

SMALL TALK - ENLIGHTENING INTERRUPTIONS

Small Talk is ... striking up a conversation with someone on a business trip and that one chance meeting changes your entire life!

8

CULTURAL AWARENESS, AGE & GENDER BIAS

"PINK" - JOY

"When you learn something from people, or from a culture, you accept it as a gift, and it is your lifelong commitment to preserve it and build on it." – Yo-Yo Ma

A good conversationalist always has available the qualities of being a chameleon - regardless of the culture, regardless of age, gender, language or social class – he or she will serenely adapt and fit in perfectly into the surroundings.

Therefore, having the ability or skill to firstly small talk in English, but perhaps also a little in German, French, Japanese and Chinese, has never been more critical in the business world today. Secondly, to be a bit more curious, aware and knowledgeable about the many (inter)cultural norms and values of the countries we are visiting, ensuring a more pleasant, enjoyable and successful stay there.

Because of the ever-increasing and significant technological advancements, companies now deal with a much larger customer base, meaning that products and services are being offered to a broader world market, outside the original country and culture of origin.

Before, it was the norm for the majority of companies, who were dealing with international customers and clients, to personally visit their customers beforehand - offering them a personal relationship - to establish trust before any contracts were signed.

Although many companies now prefer their employees to deal with other colleagues and clients via the multitude of teleconferencing platforms readily available, there is here a missing deeper level of "real" communication. Perhaps being a step too far upon this struggle for an increased optimisation of a method; a missing out on the personal touch … of actually meeting someone face-to-face and getting a "feel" about that person and the company who we want to go into business with.

This *'false optimisation'* – saving on the time and money involved by sending a representative to somewhere else; having an employee staying at an expensive hotel; and wining and dining a potential new client in the evening – is short-term saving and missing that opportunity to build trust, as talked about previously. We need to see someone – one-to-one … to know if we trust this person, the company they represent and if we want to go into business with them.

CULTURAL AWARENESS, AGE & GENDER BIAS

Cultural awareness or inter-cultural competence is ...

> *"... a range of cognitive, affective, and behavioural skills that lead to effective and appropriate communication with people of other cultures."* [39]

One of the major problems is that we consider our own language and culture as being *'the'* benchmark ... a standard to which we consider to be 'right', 'proper' and 'true'. This **ethnocentric**[40] view of culture needs to be addressed and understood when visiting other countries and cultures – and, because of this, there is now an increasing number of companies who specialise in assisting the business traveller and those who need to spend time abroad.

When researching the cultural differences between nations, it might be a little unjust to define an entire country by these attributes – either negative, positive or both. These are also "fleeting" ... as many would change over time – and so not be truly representative of the nation as a whole. Despite this, here are just a few examples:

The **Dutch**[41] are renowned for their directness. They even have a word in the Dutch language *bespreekbaarheid* or *speakability*. This might have derived from when the nation changed from Catholicism to Calvinism in the 16th century. Calvinism is a religion which promotes, amongst other things, total honesty and introspection, allowing the populations of the Netherlands to talk about everything - and only having a few taboo topics.

The **Germans**[42] are renowned throughout the world for avoiding small talk – they want to have a 'decent' conversation and not the fleeting: *"Hello!"* when out shopping or seeing a neighbour in the street. They want to be informed; they want and need information (hence the number of road signs) and this information should also be quite exact. This is totally different from the British, who are quite happy to hear that a building was built "some time" in the Middle Ages or that it is "about" 8 o'clock - and not 3 minutes to eight.

The **Swedes** apparently do not enjoy small talk with strangers, and usually, they also avoid eye-contact with others, if at all possible. If consequently, a short small talk conversation does start, it might be ended abruptly – which might be deemed rude by other nationalities.

Similar to the Swedes, many other Scandinavian countries promote the motto of "silence is golden" - perhaps owing to the lack of sunlight in the winter months. The Finns, however, are famous for their slow-paced conversations – possibly due to the complexities of the Finnish language.

The populace of the United States is mostly happy to enter into a quick small talk conversation – even if this conversation is at a somewhat superficial level. Dependent on the region, the people from the US feel it necessary to show engagement with other people they are speaking to – perhaps using head-nods and words like: *uh hum, yup, absolutely* or *awesome*. Those Americans from the Midwest and western part of the US like their conversations to be sincere, polite and mostly politically correct.

An interesting and extended comparison between nationalities and dimensions/attributes can be seen on the **Geert Hofstede Insight**[44] website – comparing two or more nations, e.g.: **The UK and Germany**.[45]

The anthropologist, **Bronisław Malinowski**[46], stated in 1923, that "purposeless" expressions such as: *"How are you today?"* or *"Have a great day."* may appear trivial or nonsensical to the situation, but they still play an essential function in bonding between participants.

Similarly, in Japanese, there is a form of phatic expression called **Aizuchi**[47] [aizuti]. These are used as interjections during conversations – which firstly, indicates that a person is actually listening; and secondly, gives reassuring sounds to the speaker that what they are saying is being understood. These generally add emphasis and understanding to the conversation being heard. These, expressions in other languages, might be seen as gesturing, smiling, the direction of looking, blushing and nodding.

A modern-day phatic expression might be seen on social media in the use of "likes", "shares" or even use of emoji. This can be seen in the work by Radovanovic and Ragnedda:

Small talk in the Digital Age: Making Sense of Phatic Posts.[48]

Speaking about the weather or the climate is normally a safe topic of discussion – albeit if the weather is usually changeable in nature. Similarly, as in Malaysia where the weather is generally always very humid and hot – and where speaking to strangers does not come naturally to most - a better small talk conversation might be the traffic or commenting about the spicy food.

Where someone's status is significant or highly regarded, such as in Japan, small talk might be used to categorise – or to allocate a hierarchical level or position. In China just approaching someone and saying: *"Hello"* or *"nǐ hǎo"* is perfectly acceptable. The topics used are the same in the English language – but are common around the area of food – where it is regarded as more of a social event.

Conversely, in China, it might be better to avoid the subjects of what you earn and border issues, such as in Taiwan and Tibet – where there have been many historical problems and concerns. Also, avoid environmental situations – climate change and pollution; any human rights issues; and even the touchy topic of animal and welfare rights.

At any rate, most Chinese find it hard to end a conversation, perhaps because it might seem abrupt or rude; for this reason, it often stops people from starting a small talk conversation in the first place.

Although it is essential to keep abreast or aware of some of the cultural differences experienced in other countries, it is almost impossible to avoid "all" of these mistakes; and making the occasional *faux pas* must be expected sometimes. Just as most languages change over time, so do the norms, values and habits of individual countries, together with the unique cultural expectations.

As mentioned previously, **Geert Hofstede**[49] was born in Haarlem, in the Netherlands and is best known for his work on cross-cultural groups and organisations. He developed the cultural dimensions theory, in which he describes the six dimensions of national culture. These are: Power & Distance, Individualism, Masculinity, Uncertainty & Avoidance, Long-term Orientation and Indulgence.

In the following video, Hofstede explains:

'the importance of an international perspective'[50]

The first is that *'we share the spoken language'*; and the second, that we act on *'shared rules and standards'*. This means that to small talk with someone – perhaps in a foreign language – we need to have the ability to use the language well, in order to adequately be able to use small talk as a means of communication.

It appears that the spoken English language seems to offer the speaker of small talk somewhat of a ... pleasant courtesy. Small talk in English often sounds softer and friendlier, compared to that of the quicker and emphatic tones and grammar of the French language - or the even more laborious and harsher German language.

If we look at the French word: **Etiquette**[51] (ᵉtikᵉt), we know it to mean an accepted code of behaviour regarding expectations for those entering into any social situation - including society, class or other groups of people.

Just as the word: "etiquette" can be something that helps us *"survive"* in a social situation, so does the term: *"cultural awareness"* when abroad. With this in mind, when we speak to someone – perhaps using the techniques suggested in this book – we need to know what is and what is not acceptable – topics and themes - when we are small-talking at any given moment in time.

Let us ponder once again the quote: *"No man is an Iland, intire of it selfe; every man is a peece of the Continent, a part of the maine."* by **John Donne**[52].

Many young people, as well as many older and supposedly wiser people, honestly believe that they can be totally independent and live without the assistance or interaction of others. For this reason, they also think that there is no need to communicate with others – especially those who they feel are "beneath" them. Yet, communication is the spice of life … it is those interactions with others that, like travel, broadens the mind.

A few questions and concerns regarding how the young are communicating with the outside world. Is the needle moving towards the young increasing in their communicative traits? Are they now more in touch with each other through social and digital media? Are they really in contact more or is this form of communication, using smart gadgets, really communication? And what about the quality of this interaction? These are issues for another day – but certainly interesting and worth further discussion or study.

An excuse from someone under 20 years of age might be: *'Why speak to someone directly when we can write someone an email or message them instantly via WhatsApp, Facebook or Instagram?'*

For those who are fearful of social interaction, the use of social media contact is undoubtedly a godsend ... for there is no "real" communication – just the electronic use of emojis and messages with little regard of spelling, grammar, etc.

In 2012, a study by Rice University concerning the use of emojis when messaging comparing men to women we can observe that ...

"Women use emoticons more than men in text messaging :-)"
[53]

Being that when women are talking to other women, their speech patterns tend to be more supportive in nature. Small talk is usually complimentary, especially regarding appearance or dress. Sharing is also more common among women. Friendly self-disclosure between women builds the foundation of friendship more, which generally unites them together in a closer bonding.

Men, on the other hand, tend to be somewhat louder and rather more competitive. There is a lot more verbal and apparently aggressive interaction, such as playfully insulting each other – as a term of endearment. However, this is typically regarded as acceptable and just banter.

Most men usually strive for perfection. This perfectionism – especially getting something "perfect" – often gets in the way of enjoying the small talk conversation. So, instead of just speaking and possibly making a mistake – some men, just do not enter into a small talk situation, for fear of "getting it wrong" and the shame involved. An unfortunate fact is that for many men, the stress of perfection is leading to an increase in **male suicide**.[54]

When speaking a non-native language, such as English, mainly it is the men who worry too much about getting the grammar correct – instead of being fluent. So, rather than saying something "less than perfect" they do not say anything at all.

The acceptability and unacceptability of small talk also differ within the many cultures of the world. The topics or themes together with the subtle rules of engagement also vary depending on the country we are visiting.

Before we move onto the next chapter, we can conclude, as previously discussed, that if we spend time learning and following any or all of the given norms, values and customs of a culture, this still might not be enough.

It may be our goal to "fit-in" and "adapt" to the visiting country and culture, - just as the chameleon does in a new environment - yet, because we are merely human, we are still sometimes bound to err and make mistakes. For this reason, we must lose our perfectionist beliefs, for if we learn from these mistakes and apologise (if possible) then the next time we will make fewer mistakes - which sums up life, as we know it to be.

CULTURAL AWARENESS, AGE & GENDER BIAS

This is how we progress ... this is the norm! This is enjoyment and pleasure. This is what life is supposed to be about!

—

Let us now go over some of the important ideas talked about in this chapter.

- **- comparing small talk to an important skill**
- **- it examines the advancement of telecommunication platforms and the ever-increasing struggle of modern optimisation**
- **- how our own language and culture can be seen as being ethnocentric**
- **- how describing nation states and cultures as being fleeting moments in time**
- **- how utterances rather than words can be important (phatic expressions)**
- **- the comparison between cultural awareness versus etiquette; the necessity of connectivity – especially with the young**
- **- how men and women communicate**
- **- how striving to be perfect can be detrimental and accepting to make a mistake or to err is normal**

SMALL TALK - ENLIGHTENING INTERRUPTIONS

Small talk is ... like journalism - we have to show interest in other people and listen to their stories!

9

TYING UP LOOSE ENDS

"BLACK" - *ENLIGHTENMENT*

"Anyone can be self-educated if they find the loose end of something to care about passionately." - Francis Spufford

Throughout this book, we have been asked to compare and contrast the many unique characteristics of the **chameleon**[55] to that of human interaction - by way of small talk and how we communicate with other people.

One may have noticed that, as this book unfolded, the earlier chapters were labelled with brighter colours, this was an illustration to indicate perhaps a possible resistance of the reader of what was being written and presented. As the book progressed, there should have been more of an acceptance, hence the darker colours towards the end of the book – these should have been not too grudgingly accepted or tolerated.

When a 'camp' of chameleons congregate, there is often a

change in skin colour or pigment – the guanine crystals under the skin, change the wavelength of light reflected off these crystals. This is often dependent on how the chameleons are feeling emotionally. Something similar can be seen or felt when humans gather in an informal meeting or social occasion - this is where the real magic can be seen and felt by all those present.

Just as a chameleon has the ability to change the colour of its skin, demonstrating its physiological state and intentions to other chameleons in its vicinity, we as humans, use the semblance of social and body signalling. However, instead of changing our skin colour – although blushing might be an exception here - we prefer to use words and body language to interact and communicate with the people who we come into contact with.

The chameleon often shows brighter skin colours - red, orange, yellow, green and turquoise - when showing aggression or hostility to other chameleons; and darker colours - light-blue, blue, purple, pink, brown or black - when being passive and contented.

As previously noted, for good small talk to occur, we need to be not only observant but also steadfast and graceful. A chameleon's eyes can move and focus independently of each other, permitting it to look at two different objects at the same time. For this reason, we, as humans, also need to be curious and alert of our surroundings, despite not having the ability to focus on two things at the same time.

Also, the chameleons rhythmically backward and forward gait

shows purposefulness, steadfastness and perhaps even grace when moving – and this is an aptitude which might be - even if appearing somewhat hesitant in nature at times – advantageous to ourselves.

Just as a chameleon is highly attentive and vigilant, we, as humans, also need to strive to be (more) curious and (more) observant, too. We also need to be (more) steady in our stance and, if possible, to avoid hesitation, general dithering and procrastination.

We generally need to be more courageous in our outlook and, perhaps more importantly, to also expand our **comfort zone**[56] whenever and wherever possible. However, this alertness should be happening in "the real world" and now, at this exact moment in time – **the Power of Now**[57] ... and not some digitalised imaginary world of what has just happened on a social media platform or a 24-hour news channel.

As indicated previously, there are two main camps when exploring the importance or significance of small talk in the modern (business) world. Either you cannot see – or want to see - the relevance of using it OR one realises that, especially in our private and professional lives, it remains incredibly important and significant. Without apologising too much, and regardless of your starting point, this book has been heavily influenced and concentrated on the benefits of the first idea.

To conclude ... if this book has still not (yet) convinced you that no (wo)man is an island and that you believe that learning small talk is not worth the time or effort, then I totally accept your decision!

We could, if wanted, devour a savoury snack hastily or greedily consume an incredible gateau, but the enjoyment involved in the consuming of such delights is far more than just providing our daily nutritional needs – it is what makes up being in our world and at this moment in time. It is authentic and adds to our whole being and our enjoyment of what we do and why we do it.

What if someone still isn't having any of it?

I have avoided being **political and spiritual**[58] until the end of this book, mainly because it frightens a lot of people in the business world, but this is something that is slowly changing and that I feel very strongly about. I talked previously about the two camps. Those that admire and use small talk to engage with others AND those that think it is a waste of time and try to avoid it.

In my other book, **Reaching Holistic Change**, I talk about being at the right place at the right time … this is called synchronicity.

The What Ifs ...
- *· What if that person, sitting alone at a table, knows something about something that you need in business?*
- *· What if that person will introduce you to someone else, meaning that you will eventually find that ideal mate?*
- *· What if he or she is actively looking for a new business idea to invest in?*

Unless we take the initiative, we will never know. What are the worst things that might happen? As mentioned at the beginning of this book, I am still keenly interested in other people ... they fascinate me as a sociologist and writer; their culture intrigues me; their uniqueness baffles me; their story makes me nosey to find out more. What an excellent opportunity to mutually grow together and perhaps become more than the sum of its social parts.

Small talk is a method or a way for me, as a writer, to learn something 'authentic' about another person. Just like my favourite travel-writer, Lawrence Durrell explained, when talking about Stendhal, that we can learn from every experience or person we meet:

"Well, the point is it was a good waste of time in some ways, but I kept an open notebook. I took an example from Stendhal, who never wasted a trick, and it all came in very useful ..."[59]

Similarly, when we are in an **interview situation,**[60] we need to show that we are not only adaptable but also friendly. Before the actual interview begins, a short small talk situation shows just how capable someone is; having the right "fit" to become the latest part of the team – a team-player or not. As an employee, the employer needs to know if you can fit into the professional culture of the company and interact with staff and clients.

A five-minute small talk chat shows the Human Relations staff just how agile we are at impromptu conversation – indicating the ability to have good rapport in times of stress. Having a good rapport relaxes the situation for all parties … this lightens the mood, and we can just relax for a moment to gather our thoughts.

When we first speak with someone that we do not know – we allow or permit a possible bonding to take place; thus, allowing the potential for something new and exciting to come into existence.

In the business world, but especially in the UK, it is vital to first talk about *"other things"* – setting the table, if you prefer, before discussing the main topic of the meeting. If someone offers us a coffee, we should always accept … as this is a healthy sign of friendship and sharing – similar to the open-hand symbolising openness.

As mentioned before, it is generally worth preparing something that we are willing and able to share with someone else … in an impromptu situation, such as in a lift or elevator.

***

I would once again at this juncture, like to make a short personal interlude, regarding my own personal story regarding being courageous and learning from other people from my childhood.

Is that person sitting alone at a table a fucking crazy person? A drunk? An axe murderer? You will not find out … unless you practise your small talk. My experience is, nevertheless, that most people you are going to meet are good, decent people that will welcome polite conversation ... and perhaps, who knows, where this will lead???

On a personal level, my late father was a twin – his twin brother was much louder and seemed to be friendlier with others; be it customers, shopkeepers, neighbours or friends. My father, on the other hand, was shy and seemed to avoid getting into conversations with others. Besides, my mother was the catalyst in my father's life. It was she who instigated contact – so that my father did not have to.

I realised early on in life, that it actually took more effort to avoid people; that speaking or saying 'hello' was easier than looking away or just ignoring the other. I had also heard about other "unsocial" people who would open the front door and quickly peer-out to see if any neighbours where outside, just to avoid the dreaded small talk situation and social interaction.

So, I guess the question raised in this book must be:

> *"Why do some people find it easier to interact with others, whereas other people find it as difficult as pulling a tooth?"*

When I was a teenager, we had two sets of famous visitors to our family home. The first was a pop band – who were getting increasing attention on tv and had recently performed their latest song on "**Top of the Pops**"[61] on the **BBC**.[62] The second was a friend of my mothers who arrived from abroad to visit for a while.

This friend was everything that my father was not. Very brash, loud and a bit of a show-off. I found him fascinating and curious – and, just like the subtitle from The X Files, **I wanted to believe**[63]. He seemed to be incredibly successful, compared to my dad, who was hardly ever there and always complaining about not having enough (although, looking back, this trait is incredibly British in nature).

I remember meeting the band members in our front room with my parents – and, realised that instead of being 'god-like' or extra special, they were just three ordinary men that admittedly had the talent to sing together and perform on stage well – but that was all. This talent was undoubtedly needed, but this was something that was not obvious at that early age. In my mind, being famous meant that these people had something "special" – something that I believed that I would never have or even deserve.

Later, while studying, I met perchance a very famous **glam-rock singer**[64] from the 1970s and 80s - who was in the company of two very young pretty women. After having a chat and a cup of tea, I realised once more that he was just an ordinary person. Unfortunately, many years later, he fell from favour and was publicly disgraced by the media.

In chapter three, I discussed how I suffered severely with stuttering. As explained later, I overcame this stuttering by using melody, in a similar way to when an opera singer uses melody to tell a story using song. My speech now, when I am teaching and under stress or duress, one can sometimes hear that my speech patterns are very melodic in nature. And when

I go online to teach my students, I still turn on the webcam 'after' I have got the first words out of my mouth.

***

At work, **collegiality** has become even more critical in our daily working lives – hence the emphasis on being a team player. We are kept busy and are increasingly being asked to do more and more.

Having good colleagues at these times of stress and overwork to assist us can be a godsend. This goes to show that, if we are well-liked and to be known as friendly within our own department or company - and we one day need some help to complete something - then the chances are that one of our colleagues will help us when we need them to. On the other hand, if we consider ourselves to be *"an island"* and if we are seen as unfriendly, discourteous or rude to other colleagues – then chances are they will not help us.

Another great reason for practising our art – even if we consider ourselves shy or introverted – is that we will no longer have to avoid those awkward company events and social engagements. We will be able to "better fit in" with other colleagues at the Christmas party, mainly because we will be able to really enjoy the gathering and will not feel the previous intimidation experienced beforehand. This is how using small talk can easily expand our comfort zone.

We have to remember that, when we share a piece of information with someone – perhaps something small but personal, we have to see what that person does with this information. Do they spread it around with other people or does it remain private? This is how wonderful, long-term relationships are cultivated and grown.

Once there is good common ground, small talk can then be replaced or exchanged with something more substantial and something that we both know and care about. Although, when meeting that person again at a later date, we still need to "test the water" with a little small talk to get things going once again – just in case, things have changed.

So, regardless of the social variables, for example; social status, ethnicity, religion, level of education, age, or gender, etc.) small talk should always be achievable and possible in most circumstances.

We are, as humans, incredibly inquisitive and because of this, we are also always pushing our limits and boundaries to find out "more". In contrast, and just like the myth of **Pandora's Box**[66], we are told to be cautious and taught not to tamper with things that we are unfamiliar with; despite having a burning desire of being curious, together with having the necessary and unfathomable desire of human enquiry.

My own research has indicated that one of the main reasons why the English language appears to be easier and lighter in tone when doing small talk, is first, that there is no longer a differentiation between the informal "Tu/Du/Thou" and the more formal "Vous/Sie/You" found in the English language. And second, the melody of the English language mimics

the rhythm of our heart[67].

This addressing someone using the formal "YOU" found in French and German - used when we speak to someone who we either do not know or someone older than ourselves - "demarcates social distance" and is generally used to keep someone at arm's length or/and showing someone respect. In England, this formal 'you-ness' was gradually phased out during the 15th and 16th century – making way for the informal "you" which can be 'seen' and 'felt' as more neutral and perhaps even welcoming.

My French and German students often ask about using "you" to show respect. The English language also offers a few ways of showing respect – perhaps for a client or customer. We use a more elaborated form to *Vous* or *Sie* someone:

"Excuse me, Dr. Smith, may I interrupt? Would now be a good time to serve the light refreshments? Would you care to have your coffee now or perhaps later?" (formal)

versus:

"Shall we break for coffee now, Bob?" (informal)

The English language lends itself more to a light conversation and this is perhaps why it is now the dominant business language worldwide – despite the dominance of China or Korea - and formally Japan.

***

My wishes and expectations in the completion of this book – together perhaps more importantly ... with you reading its pages and understanding its message – is that you will enjoy your next small talk encounter more and, at the same time, to confirm my **raison d'être**[68] and make this a **self-fulfilling prophecy**.[69]

I pride myself – as a transformative coach and trainer - in the knowledge that I "care" about the students I teach and the clients I work with on a regular basis. For this reason, I hope that you will always remember the following:

- - small talk can offer friendship
- - it may intensify the understanding of someone else or even an unfamiliar culture
- - it could show your respect for another - for no better reason than offering the hand of friendship to someone else before beginning with the real reason for coming together.

This is building a relationship with my students – perhaps through small talk; probably by being incredibly curious; maybe me being nosey? My students 'feel' the trust that we have built up over many years. They are happy to tell me how they are feeling – because they know that I am not going to judge them but just listen – and hopefully remember. If I remember something about them ... perhaps in a small talk conversation ... and use it next time, then they naturally feel "understood", and their existence is confirmed and heightened in our time together.

It is a large part of giving and taking – and mutual respect. Occasionally I ask my students if they would like a different teacher or trainer – mainly because our relationship has perhaps run-its-course; perhaps as there is no longer that ability for them to grow. This is generally okay for me, because as a teacher, I need to allow for this growth to take place and to finally let my students move on.

Perhaps we should consider changing our mindset. Instead of thinking *"I am an island"* we need to be something kinder and warmer, maybe more like: "I am curious, tell me more?"

And finally, before we end this book – which has really been a lot of fun to write (he lied ;)) – let us talk briefly about the **Imposter Syndrome**[70]. Most people – even experts or people who hold high positions in society – occasionally explain that during a speech or standing in front of a group of people – they think a thought such as:

"Shit! Shit! I have no idea about what I am saying. I am an imposter ... I am not an expert. What the hell am I doing here?"

Now, compare this with the **Dunning-Kruger effect.**[71] This is when people with low ability/intelligence have mistaken superiority and assess their own cognitive ability as greater than it actually is.

Bertrand Russell[72], the philosopher and mathematician who once said:

"One of the painful things about our time is that those who feel certainty are stupid, and those with any imagination and understanding are filled with doubt and indecision."

Finally, during my research for this book, one story highlights the advantages of having the courage to enter into a small talk situation. The person in question always greeted someone at her workplace who always looked sad and grumpy. Moreover, she persevered with little or no positive response.

Then one day, when she was herself feeling sad, angry and frustrated, this normally grumpy employee passed her in the corridor and greeted her with a smile and a short conversation until the lift arrived at their floor. **What goes around – comes around**:[73] proving the proverb that the consequences of one's actions will have to be dealt with eventually, sometimes called Karma.

We should also understand that getting something "perfect" – using struggle, is generally, not only impossible most of the time but that there is no fun or enjoyment in the process of doing something. Enjoying what we do, perhaps with passion, on a daily basis, is the contrast to stress, burnout and depression.

So, if English is not our first language and we say to someone on holiday: *"How many costs this?"* The person hearing this instinctively "knows" exactly what we want and what we are talking about. This highlights that even if we realise that this sentence is not exactly correct – we still understand what is trying to be said.

We have to purposely forget about negative past events – which perhaps linger and haunt us into the present. Be that the time when we spoke to someone on holiday and we were rudely snubbed. And remember more about the small positive moments, when our chambermaid who just wanted to thank us - using two sentences in fluent Mallorquin Spanish - for the money left for her in our room, who, after realising that I didn't understand – just said: *Gracias* and a smile.

-

The writing and publishing of this book has been my own selfish plea to others, to change our world in some small but significant way. My hope is that the next time you see someone sitting alone, be brave and approach that person with an open hand and a smile! Who knows where this interaction will take you. Who knows if this small act of kindness will change something, not just for you, but perhaps for that other person as well. Most who are feeling lost or lonely just want to be understood and listened to - without having an argument, having advice stuffed down their throat or told what to do. Many are living a secret life of 'ever so quiet' desperation, and by you taking the initiative using small talk to get the ball rolling, this might just be enough to prevent them feeling alone and lost.

Thank you!

Antony xxx

REFERENCES

1. Hyperlinks - From Wikipedia
   https://en.wikipedia.org/wiki/Hyperlink

2. The courage of a lion - YouTube "Courage"
   https://www.youtube.com/watch?v=LEEyijiTW-I

3. Brexit breakdown: southern discomfort | Anywhere but Westminster
   https://youtu.be/ZwbYjgL0qdA?t=55

4. Huis Clos (No Exit) -Wikipedia
   https://en.wikipedia.org/wiki/No_Exit

5. Stuttering and Stammering - wikipedia
   https://en.wikipedia.org/wiki/Stuttering#cite_note-33

6. Stuttering and Cluttering: Frameworks for understanding treatment
   https://www.amazon.com/dp/B074TSPMS2

7. The King's Speech - Film Wikipedia
   https://en.wikipedia.org/wiki/The_King%27s_Speech

REFERENCES

8. Phatic Expressions - Forbes
   https://www.forbes.com/sites/markmurphy/2016/12/04/heres-the-phatic-expression-you-should-never-say-to-remote-employees

9. One Woman, 17 British Accents - Anglophenia Ep 5 - YouTube
   https://youtu.be/FyyT2jmVPAk

10. Weak Forms - How to Pronounce Weak Forms in English

https://youtu.be/31-xVBwGNDY

11. The Schwa - Wikipedia
    https://en.wikipedia.org/wiki/Schwa

12. The myth of Pandora's Box – TED Talk
    https://www.ted.com/talks/iseult_gillespie_the_myth_of_pandora_s_box?language=en

13. Facebook/Cambridge Analytica – The Guardian
    https://www.theguardian.com/news/2018/mar/17/cambridge-analytica-facebook-influence-us-election

13a. Data Harvesting - The Guardian
    https://www.theguardian.com/us-news/2015/dec/11/senator-ted-cruz-president-campaign-facebook-user-data

14. Chameleon Changing Color - YouTube
    https://youtu.be/ioblgpA5eTo

15. They put a homeless man in a suit and he asks for money on the streets - YouTube
    https://youtu.be/c6uif8OKGZ8

16. Civil Inattention - Wikipedia
    https://en.wikipedia.org/wiki/Civil_inattention

17. LA BISE by PAUL TAYLOR (VOSTFR) - YouTube
    https://youtu.be/T-VWbV6TJxU

18. 'The Triple Brezhnev': A Legendary Kiss
    https://youtu.be/YX-QW2vfNtY

19. The Cocktail Party Effect - Wikipedia
    https://bit.ly/1K7uaeN

20. How To Smile At Women And Make Them Want You - YouTube
    https://youtu.be/tm_WPB4Qrww

21. TRUMP Owns Macron (And His Wife) in an INSANE 30 Second Handshake Battle - YouTube
    https://bit.ly/2GFp3qN

22. 29 Second Handshake – Trump/Macron - YouTube
    https://www.youtube.com/watch?v=1DwijJfVbBg

23. BBC Radio 4 Shipping Forecast 09/04/2014 - YouTube
    https://youtu.be/mSq4nfH4y6Q?t=168

24. The Durrells in Corfu, Season 2: Episode 1 Scene - YouTube

https://youtu.be/OrtzcxumknU

25. Theories of Human Communication - Littlejohn 2002 - Amazon
https://www.amazon.com/Theories-Human-Communication-Stephen-Littlejohn-ebook/dp/B01NBHPNAR

26. Theoretical Studies Towards a Sociology of Language – Bernstein 1971 - Amazon
https://www.amazon.com/Theoretical-Studies-Towards-Sociology-Language-dp-0415302870/dp/0415302870

27. Elaborated Code and Restricted Code - Wikipedia
https://en.wikipedia.org/wiki/Basil_Bernstein#Elaborated_code_and_restricted_code

28. Open-Ended Questions- Wikipedia
https://en.wikipedia.org/wiki/Open-ended_question

29. Closed-Ended Questions - Wikipedia
https://en.wikipedia.org/wiki/Closed-ended_question

30. Active Listening - Wikipedia
https://en.wikipedia.org/wiki/Active_listening

31. Reflective Listening - Wikipedia
https://en.wikipedia.org/wiki/Reflective_listening

32. Empathetic Listening
https://goalbookapp.com/toolkit/strategy/active-listening

33. We tend to meet disclosure with disclosure, even with strangers. - TED Talk
   https://www.ted.com/talks/kio_stark_why_you_should_talk_to_strangers

34. My Fair Lady - The Rain in Spain - YouTube
   https://youtu.be/xmADMB2utAo?t=36

35. Catch Me if you Can – Nobody's Chasing You - YouTube
   https://youtu.be/sFW15hEqZQk

36. Speed Dating - Wikipedia
   https://en.wikipedia.org/wiki/Speed_dating

37. Flirting - Wikipedia
   https://en.wikipedia.org/wiki/Flirting

38. Elevator Speech - Wikipedia
   https://en.wikipedia.org/wiki/Elevator_pitch

39. Intercultural competence - Wikipedia
   https://en.wikipedia.org/wiki/Intercultural_competence

40. Ethnocentrism - Wikipedia
   https://en.wikipedia.org/wiki/Ethnocentrism

41. The Dutch - BBC
   http://www.bbc.com/travel/story/20180131-where-dutch-directness-comes-from

42. The Germans - YouTube

https://youtu.be/539n0ahI0Ts

43. The Swedes - hejsweden
https://hejsweden.com/en/small-talk-with-swedes/

44. Geert Hofstede Insight
https://www.hofstede-insights.com/

45. The UK and Germany
https://www.hofstede-insights.com/country-comparison/germany,the-uk/

46. Bronisław Malinowski - Wikipedia
https://en.wikipedia.org/wiki/Bronis%C5%82aw_Malinowski

47. Aizuchi - frequent interjections in Japanese - Wikipedia
https://en.wikipedia.org/wiki/Aizuchi

48. Small talk in the Digital Age: Making Sense of Phatic Posts by Radovanovic and Ragnedda - eprints
http://eprints.rclis.org/24377/1/paper_18.pdf

49. Geert Hofstede - Wikipedia
https://en.wikipedia.org/wiki/Geert_Hofstede

50. The importance of an international perspective - YouTube
https://youtu.be/4mpcyxSdUcw

51. Etiquette - Wikipedia
https://en.wikipedia.org/wiki/Etiquette

52. John Donne - Wikipedia
   https://en.wikipedia.org/wiki/John_Donne

53. Women use emoticons more than men in text messaging :-) - Rice University
   http://news.rice.edu/2012/10/10/women-use-emoticons-more-than-men-in-text-messaging/

54. Male perfectionism and suicide - Psypost
   https://www.psypost.org/2015/05/the-male-suicides-how-social-perfectionism-kills-men-34574

55. The Chameleon - Wikipedia
   https://en.wikipedia.org/wiki/Chameleon

56. Comfort Zone - Wikipedia
   https://en.wikipedia.org/wiki/Comfort_zone

57. The Power of Now – Eckhart Tolle - Wikipedia
   https://en.wikipedia.org/wiki/The_Power_of_Now

58. Understanding the 'why' in business - Forbes
   https://www.forbes.com/sites/stanphelps/2017/04/10/understanding-your-why-in-business-through-the-eight-purpose-archetypes/#6e2ed2363564

59. But I kept an open notebook - Google Books
   http://bit.ly/2UXB1xW

60. Interview Situation - Top Interview
   https://www.topinterview.com/interview-advice/job-

interview-small-talk

61. Top of the Pops - Wikipedia
https://en.wikipedia.org/wiki/Top_of_the_Pops

62. The BBC - Wikipedia
https://en.wikipedia.org/wiki/BBC

63. X Files – I want to believe - Wikipedia
https://en.wikipedia.org/wiki/The_X-Files:_I_Want_to_Believe

64. Glam-Rock - Wikipedia
https://en.wikipedia.org/wiki/Gary_Glitter

65. Collegiality - Wikipedia
https://en.wikipedia.org/wiki/Collegiality

66. Pandora's Box - Wikipedia
https://en.wikipedia.org/wiki/Pandora%27s_box

67. Rhythm of the Heart – The Guardian
https://www.theguardian.com/education/2015/mar/06/feel-the-beat-how-rhythm-shapes-the-way-we-use-and-understand-language

68. Raison d'être – the meaning of life - Wikipedia
https://en.wiktionary.org/wiki/raison_d%27%C3%AAtre#English

69. Self-Fulfilling Prophecy - Wikipedia

https://en.wikipedia.org/wiki/Self-fulfilling_prophecy

70. Imposter Syndrome - Wikipedia
https://en.wikipedia.org/wiki/Impostor_syndrome

71. Dunning-Kruger Effect - Wikipedia
https://en.wikipedia.org/wiki/Dunning%E2%80%93Kruger_effect

72. Bertrand Russell - Wikipedia
https://en.wikipedia.org/wiki/Bertrand_Russell

73. What goes around - YouTube
https://youtu.be/unzWJWiCALA

—

Cover Photo - by Kuttelvaserova Stuchelova Shutterstock

About the Author

Coach Antony (Antony Birks) is a transformative executive coach and Business English trainer and teacher. He has, over the past 30 years, been mentoring and coaching a diverse international audience.

Coming from a working-class area of London, and at the age of 30, he left England with his Bachelor of Science and moved to Germany – a place that he enjoyed as a child and now the place he calls home. His goal and role as a coach and teacher - after having experienced losing everything that was dear to him - is to now bring "the best out" of the people who he works with – with this being a passion; meaning that, most of the time, it certainly does not feel like "work" in the normal sense to him.

Coach Antony is best known for his book: "One Hundred and

One Daily Challenges and Affirmations: Helping to Find Inner Peace and Happiness in Daily Life", which is widely regarded as offering suggested thoughts about life to those with little or no time in our apparent hectic and fast-moving society.

Coach Antony is now, once again rising from the ashes. This rise, fall and rise has made him re-examine once again his passion with a new light. Being in the third stage, from within Joseph Campbell's Hero's Journey, this puts him in the last section – The Return ... where he now wishes to share his "treasure" with this international audience; enlightened readers; and others ... who are just willing to listen and perhaps learn.

He now lives, writes and teaches in Hannover, Germany. His sense of purpose – his *raison d'être* – is now mainly concentrated on his aptitude to teach; his further curiosity to study sociological, psychological and philosophical change; and his general passion to write. His lifelong experiences have highlighted for him what is now important and what is no longer important.

His profound yet taken-for-granted teachings and suggestions have assisted an international audience to gently find solutions ... where they were hidden or masked beforehand.

Antony is a kindly spoken but prolific public speaker and writer, addressing organisations and companies using his directness and giving his alternative keynote speeches.

If you have enjoyed this book ... please leave me a review ...

here:
https://amzn.to/2sojraX

You can connect with me on:
- https://coachantony.wordpress.com
- http://twitter.com/coachantony
- https://www.facebook.com/enlightening-interruptions
- https://www.linkedin.com/in/antonybirks
- https://www.youtube.com/user/coachantony

Also by Coach Antony Birks

Coach Antony (Antony Birks) is a transformative executive coach and Business English trainer and teacher. He has, over the past 30 years, been mentoring and coaching a diverse international audience ... and from all structural levels - from those who work on the shop-floor, to middle managers, top executives and CEOs.

Antony is a kindly spoken but prolific public speaker and writer, addressing organisations and companies using his directness and giving his alternative keynote speeches.

One Hundred and One Daily Challenges and Affirmations:
https://www.amazon.com/One-Hundred-Daily-Challenges-Affirmations-ebook/dp/B00584WERK

This book has been carefully designed to offer the reader One Hundred and One Daily Challenges and Affirmations to assist in helping them find inner peace and happiness in daily life.

In today's busy and hectic society some find it hard to manage and get to grips with their time limitations; their relationship problems; their spirituality; their career and wealth issues; their health concerns; plus dealing with other general life issues - which seem to crop up at the most inopportune moments.

It is important to first remember that trying to quickly change a feeling or emotion – once it has gained momentum – is almost always impossible. For this reason, if you are hurting because of loss, pain, other recent traumatic events, diagnosis, etc. we have to first find a quiet, new place to calm those stormy seas and thoughts.

The hard but simple truth is ... we have to feel appreciation for the life we have lived; we have to acknowledge that there is a process going on; we have to accept that we are part of this process; that this process is perfect and that everything is unfolding perfectly (and to plan); and that nothing is going wrong and that things, all things, are always working out for you.

We have to slow the momentum down before we can begin going in the opposite, positive and new direction and that ultimately this resistance is slowing down the whole process of positive change.

Every one of the challenges assists the reader to reconsider certain important aspects of their lives – the wisdom gained is important if we are to live a fulfilled and wholesome life.

This book is to support all those who are looking to find their unique path forward and to lead them towards a life of inner peace and serenity.

Reaching Holistic Change:
https://www.amazon.com/Reaching-Holistic-Change-well-being-fallibility-ebook/dp/B07D7PZJHN

This book examines and offers a holistic approach – dealing with our place in the world; making more time; allowing for well-being; accepting our fallibility; finding and following our passion: and finally finding our reason for being in the world.

Reaching Holistic Change examines and discusses the following ideas:

Where Are You?
Where Do You Want To Go?
Understanding Momentum
Seven Suggestions to Self Care
Many Paths
Soothing Words
Meditation
Finding your Passion
and
Stop Digging your Hole

Also discussed are the areas of: Nutrition, Hydration, Body Weight, Exercise, Burnout, Stress, Company Loyalty, Technology, Self-Esteem, Self-Efficacy, Empowerment and Handling Depression.

To summarise, we need to listen more closely to our inner being or intuition and to find a powerful excuse or reason to halt these circular and repeated patterns of negative thought. Searching for answers, to an unattainable solution, or using logic at these times of severe stress and worry, is generally not helpful or useful, because the mechanism behind our thoughts, via your mind, are corrupt, and as so, functioning inadequately and being mostly ineffective and certainly unreliable.

The negative effects of stress and burnout on the modern worker, and consequentially the company he or she works for, lingers on and plays havoc with every aspect of the organisation, but especially its own success and reputation. We have to consider if we just want to deal with the 'symptoms' of stress and burnout; or if we want to handle and use the more complicated preventative suggested measures laid out in this book?

Reaching Holistic Change highlights political, environmental and cognitive change ... and, more importantly, how to come to terms with radical change in the modern world using a holistic approach.

"... empowerment has also led us down a foggy path ... muddying the borders between work and home life, and as so, has interfered with the normal, old-fashioned parameters of what is considered as having a "normal" and healthy work-life balance."

Coach Antony, offering a dynamic and exciting set of principles; sharing new, practical and useful hints and suggestions;

together with expressing his unique and unconventional way of living and surviving our ever-changing world; offers a clear and straightforward approach to change and change-making for both the private and the business world.

This book is presented and should be read like two old loyal friends having an amicable chat, perhaps over a glass of wine and in front of an open fire, with smiles; slight disagreements; and interesting, but differing observations and points of view.

The book concludes, with comparing our lives to that of a boat within a harbour. However, we have to realise and accept that boats are not made or designed to remain within the safety of the harbour walls forever. It is the raison d'être of ships and boats to sail out amongst the waves, tackling both stormy and calm weather and finally to experience and reach new and amazing places.

www.ingramcontent.com/pod-product-compliance
Lightning Source LLC
Chambersburg PA
CBHW072211170526
45158CB00002BA/549